The Young Country Doctor Book 12
Bilbury Joys

Vernon Coleman

Another collection of memories from the English village of Bilbury.

Note: As usual, names and details of individuals, animals and establishments have been altered to protect the innocent, the guilty and the somewhere in-between.

The Author

Vernon Coleman is a *Sunday Times* bestselling author. He has written over 100 books which have been translated into 25 languages and sold in over 50 countries. His books have sold over two million copies in the UK alone. Vernon Coleman is also a qualified doctor. He lives in Bilbury, Devon, England. He is an accomplished bar billiards player (three times runner up in the Duck and Puddle Christmas competition), a keen but surprisingly ineffective skittle player and an accomplished maker of paper aeroplanes. He claims to be one of the best stone skimmers in North Devon. (Nine bounces are by no means unheard of, and he once spent forty-five minutes diving in chilly coastal water in an attempt to find the beautifully proportioned flat stone with which he had achieved a personal best of 12 bounces.) He is a long-term member of the Desperate Dan Pie-Eater's Club (vegetarian section). He does not speak any foreign languages and although he can juggle, he cannot knit. He has never jumped out of an aeroplane (with or without a parachute) but he has, on several occasions, lit bonfires in the rain and is particularly proud of the fact that he once managed to light one in a snowstorm. He is tall and must still be growing for he has now burst through his hair and has a rapidly developing bald patch. He has not yet availed himself of the opportunities offered by social media but details of his surgery opening hours can be seen on the noticeboard outside Peter Marshall's shop in the village.

The Young Country Doctor series

This is the 12th book in the series. All the books in the series are available as e-books on Amazon.

Dedication

To Antoinette: then, now and eternally.

You are the only past I remember, the only present that matters and the only future I want.

Foreword

I can't imagine not living in Bilbury.

I've lived in quite a number of cities and towns, both in and outside England, and I have visited and stayed in a good many more.

Some of those places have been beautiful, some striking, some full of vitality and some almost frightening in their intensity. And in all of them, of course, there have been many fascinating, exciting and kindly people. (Of the others, we will say nothing.)

But, although I have done a little travelling, I cannot now imagine living anywhere but Bilbury. Occasionally, people from outside the village say things like 'Don't you get bored living in the same place all the time?' or 'Isn't life in a small village rather dull?' or 'Don't you miss having theatres, opera houses, museums and galleries on your doorstep?'

The answer is always a simple and honest 'No'. I never get bored in Bilbury and life in our village is anything but dull. It's true that we don't have theatres, museums and all those other places but, as a rule, we also don't have large and endless traffic jams, constant noise or air so thick with pollutants that you could cut it into cubes and store it in a cupboard.

In Bilbury we have time to think, to reflect and to look around at our wonderful world. Trees can spread their roots, plants can bloom without being choked and at some times of the year you can, if you know what to look for, pick a snack from the hedgerow as you walk from one place to another. I always think the same is true for people: we can spread our roots and bloom without fear of being choked. Living in Bilbury, I always feel that I am at home and on holiday at the same time.

The fact is, of course, that we were all originally country dwellers. We lived in hamlets and villages or, sometimes, in isolated communities which consisted of no more than one or two houses and which could not, therefore, be described as hamlets.

When the writer Daniel Defoe toured England in 1724, researching his book, *A Tour Through the Whole Island of Great*

Britain, the whole country was mainly rural. At least eight out of ten people lived in hamlets and villages – most of which had only a few hundred people living in them.

(Incidentally, at the time of Defoe's travels, the North Devon town of Barnstaple was spelt Barnstable – just like the town in the United States which shares the same name. It is, it seems, the American spelling which is the correct version. According to Defoe, the town which is now known as Bideford used to be called Biddiford and the seaside resort known as Ilfracombe was known to him as Ilfar-comb.)

Towns and cities are a relatively new development and, in historical terms, most of us have very little real cultural experience of town life. Most of us are, at heart, country dwellers who have still not properly adapted to the restrictions of town or city life. Despite this, most of us live in towns and cities. We are crammed together in blocks of flats and in rows of terraced houses. The only bits of greenery most people see are the few plants growing in window boxes, the neat, little parks and gardens where the trees are grey, the weeds ripped out before they have a chance to flower and the grass stunted and brown.

Even in the suburbs, we are often closer together than we like to be. Gardens are over-tended and anything resembling a wild flower is torn up. Nettle patches have been replaced with summerhouse decking, and patios and hedges have been ripped out and replaced with factory made fencing that doesn't need trimming. Wildlife stands no chance. The absence of wild flowers means that butterflies and bees are a rarity. Grey Squirrels are caught and bludgeoned to death because they are officially regarded as pests.

The people who designed our towns and cities used to plant trees along the roadside edges, so that we would be reminded of our rural roots by the sight of an occasional leaf. Today's planners and councillors are ripping out the trees. They say that leaves and roots are a health and safety hazard, that clearing away the leaves in autumn costs money and that dripping sap from trees damages car paintwork. Oak trees drop acorns and horse chestnut trees drop conkers – more health and safety hazards.

But we have always been basically country dwellers and most of us are, in our hearts, still country dwellers. And even if our daily lives require us to live and work in towns and cities, humans still harbour a fondness for rural living.

I know I am lucky to be able to spend my days in Bilbury, where nettles grow freely, where butterflies still flutter, where the sight of a raven is nothing unusual and where wild orchids grow freely on the untrimmed verges beneath the hedgerows.

And where the people still have time to stop and say 'hello' to one another, where door keys are lost and never missed, where cold winter days are warmed by the smell of wood smoke and where we have the time, the freedom, the patience to enjoy one other's idiosyncrasies without the instant judgements which seem to be a part of modern life.

I hope you enjoy this new volume of memories from Bilbury. These tales are all set in the 1970s but, I promise you faithfully, Bilbury has not changed since then; and I know it never will. Bilbury is forever, and, whether you are passing through, staying a while or planning to join us here permanently you will be forever welcome.

Living in Bilbury is a real joy.

Vernon Coleman, Bilbury

The Dinner Party

The Pinchbecks live in a 15th century house which was built by one of North Devon's early mine owners. It has, inevitably, been extended on many occasions and is now a large, comfortable house which offers a number of different architectural styles. From many of the rooms, and the extensive grounds, there are splendid views of the Severn Estuary and the southern coastline of the proud and independent nation of Wales which lies across the water.

At the time of which I write, Mr Pinchbeck, who was in his 50s, was a bank manager in Barnstaple. He exuded calm, dignity and presence. His wife was in her 30s and the headmistress of a local primary school. They had twins, who were aged seven or eight-years-old.

Their one weaknesss, if weakness it was, was that they shared an affection for parties. It didn't seem to matter what sort of party it was as long as it was a party. They threw parties for their children, for their relatives for their friends and for themselves. They threw parties to show off, they threw parties to celebrate good news and they threw parties to help them forget bad news. Some people believe that arnica is a cure for all ills. Others have faith in yoga. The Pinchbecks put their faith in parties. If they had been on the Titanic on its final and fatal voyage, they would have doubtless spent their last hours organising a party.

And one spring they decided to host an extravagant dinner party for a select group of friends from around the country.

It was not to be an ordinary dinner party. It was to be something they would all remember for years to come. It was to be a dinner party for gourmands; people who could eat for England; trenchermen and women who knew when they had eaten enough but never let that stop them eating more. This was not, and there was never any doubt about it, a meeting of gourmets. These were not individuals who could taste a sauce and tell you whether it contained enough basil or needed a pinch more horseradish. These were people who liked to eat and who liked to eat to excess. These were definitely gourmands, rather than gourmets; they were the sort of people who would complain that the chips are too greasy but would, nevertheless, happily chomp their way through the lot (and probably eat some of yours too). A gourmand is someone who can keep eating when he is no longer hungry. Indeed, for a gourmand, hunger and food have nothing whatsoever to do with each other.

I knew about the party long before it happened. When you live in a small village, there are always rumours, and secrets don't last very long – they tend to have the sort of life expectancy that would make a mayfly feel rather ancient.

Much of the food that was going to be served at the Pinchbecks' party had been ordered from Peter Marshall's shop and I wouldn't like to say that Peter is a gossip, not in the unpleasant sense of the word, but he does sometimes enjoy sharing information; indeed, I rather think he regards it as a duty to act as our local news provider. Moreover, there was no doubt that his newly appointed estate agent specialist, Hilda Musbury, shared his view on this.

Peter himself told me that Mrs Pinchbeck was planning to serve a number of dishes based on recipes devised by the world's greatest chefs including Brillat-Savarin, La Chapelle, Marin, Nicolas de Bonnefons and le Marechal de Richelieu. Peter said that he'd had to import 70-year-old oysters, known as pieds de cheval, from Cancale on the Brittany coast. The gourmands were, after all, going to give their taste buds a treat.

There were to be five guests at the party; all of whom had very highly developed and well-tended egos. They were individuals who had no doubt whatsoever that they were exceptional, human beings. They had, like their male half of their hosts, all motored comfortably into their fifties.

Balfour Morrison, was a schoolteacher at a well-known public school and considered himself widely known for his role as a regular guest on a BBC arts programme. He had cultivated a rich, mid-Atlantic bass voice which he felt suited his position as an arbiter of highbrow taste.

Topham Beauclerk ran a small bookshop in Exeter and specialised in dealing in old maps. He had written and self-published a small guidebook for those eager to enter this rather esoteric field. He was also an enthusiastic amateur dentist who had invented a type of rubber crown which he claimed would revolutionise life for bruxism sufferers. Sadly, however, the dental profession, fearful of losing a good deal of repeat crown work, had refused to accept his invention and Beauclerk remained embittered and rather resentful.

Both Morrison and Beauclerk were life-long bachelors.

The third guest, Claude Templeton, managed a bank in Somerset, and was a keen but inexpert golfer who was so accustomed to losing to his wealthy customers that even when he was playing alone he still managed to play rather ineptly. He considered himself to be an expert on Conan Doyle's books about the adventures of Sherlock Holmes. Templeton was married to a magazine editor who, when not working, spent most of her life tucked into a small flat in the Paddington area of London. She spent her evenings working as a Marriage Guidance Counsellor. Neither the Pinchbecks nor the other guests had ever met her and she was, indeed, something of a stranger to Claude.

The other two guests were the Chattertons; another two halves of a married couple.

Constance and Elmore Chatterton ran a small chain of sporting goods stores which were distributed throughout the West Country. They lived in a small manor house on the outskirts of Taunton. Elmore's grandfather, an expert toboggan enthusiast, who had won cups in St Moritz, had founded the first store back in the 1920s and Elmore's father had built up the business. Constance, a keen horsewoman, had won rosettes, medals and cups in dressage events. She was also an enthusiastic singer who knew and could sing the entire canon of work produced by Gilbert and Sullivan (including the male roles). Elmore, who had weighed 12 stones when he was 12-years-old could have won medals and cups if any had been available for eating. (When younger he had, indeed, won prizes in a couple of pie eating competitions.)

The Pinchbecks had at one point considered including a stranger in their dinner party (according to some old customs it is good luck to have a stranger at the dining table since there is always a chance that the stranger might well be an angel) but they had reluctantly abandoned this idea when they realised that they could not think of any strangers they wanted to invite to their home. (There had, of course, never been any chance of their inviting an actual real stranger to the party.)

11

To the astonishment of everyone in the village, it was rumoured, quite accurately, that the dinner party was designed to consist of a single meal that would last for a minimum of 12 hours and would consist of 55 separate courses. The number of courses had apparently been chosen to celebrate the fact that Mr Pinchbeck was about to celebrate his 55th birthday. Mrs Harrison, a cook from Combe Martin who usually worked at one of the local public houses, had been hired to help with the cooking and her 19-year-old son, Eric, had been hired to help with the waiting on and the washing up.

Each guest had been invited to pay £20 each towards the cost of the feast and to bring three bottles of wine to help with the digestive processes. Elmore Chatterton had, uninvited, brought with him a 12-gauge shotgun with which he was determined to 'bag a pheasant, a partridge or a couple of plump pigeons'. He had not made it clear what he intended to do with anything he succeeded in shooting.

On the Saturday of the Pinchbecks' party, I decided to sort through the old paperwork cluttering up the cupboards and shelves in my consulting room. I have always found that dated and unnecessary paperwork accumulates terribly easily. If I kept every receipt, guarantee and warning I am told to keep, I would need an aircraft hangar for storage.

I enjoyed the clear-out so thoroughly that when I had finished tidying my study, I moved around the house, doing the same thing in the drawing room, the kitchen, the butler's pantry, the cupboards in the hall, the bedrooms and even the garage. I extended my spring-clean to cover other items; not just bits of paper. Having checked with Patsy that the selected items were surplus to requirements, I sorted them into three piles. Some items I put aside for the next village jumble sale, some I put into our dustbin, so that they could be collected by the weekly bin-men, and some, by far the greatest quantity, I piled up in cardboard boxes and old shopping bags to take down the garden to our bonfire site.

By the time I'd finished, it was late morning and I had accumulated a modest amount of rubbish for the dustbin, a decent amount of unwanted stuff which I could donate to the jumble sale and a huge pile of burnable rubbish.

As I carried the boxes and old bags down the garden, I found myself looking forward to the bonfire I would have later. I had, as always, a good pile of old garden clippings and there was no doubt that I would be able to have a pretty spectacular blaze.

I sometimes suspect that I must have been an arsonist in a previous life because there are few things I enjoy more than a good bonfire. I don't know why. I can't explain it. But it is a fact of life. Some men like collecting Spode china. Some become excited if they catch a trout. I get a kick out of setting fire to a large pile of rubbish and watching it reduce to a pile of ashes. It is a bonus that the ash so produced makes an excellent contribution to the garden.

I had piled up the first bundle of rubbish, a mixture of paper and garden cuttings, and had crumpled up a few sheets of old newspaper which I had placed at the bottom of the pile when I heard Patsy calling me.

With some reluctance, I left the bonfire and hurried up the garden. I assumed at first that Patsy was calling me because luncheon was ready.

But it wasn't lunch.

'Mrs Pinchbeck called,' said Patsy. 'She wants to know if you'd pop over to their house. Their dinner party is well under way and one of the guests has been taken ill.'

I looked at my watch. 'It's only quarter to twelve!' I pointed out. I followed her back towards the house.

'I know,' agreed Patsy. 'Mrs Pinchbeck explained that because they're having a 55 course meal, they started it with a sort of brunch at 10.00 this morning. Apparently, the plan is that they will eat their way right through until 10.00 tonight. They're going to have a 30 minute break at 2.00 p.m. and another 30 minute break at 6.00 p.m. but otherwise they'll be eating for twelve hours.'

'Fifty five courses in twelve hours? That's nearly five courses an hour!' It seemed a long time to sit down eating. You could travel half way around the world in that amount of time. I shuddered at the thought of it all. In the days when I used to spend time away from Bilbury, touring round the country visiting radio and television stations, I used to get impatient if I went to a restaurant and had to sit and spend an hour on a meal. My friends Frank and Gilly Parsons, who run the Duck and Puddle, our local public house, always try to serve up my food within five minutes of receiving my order.

'I gather some of the courses are quite small,' said Patsy. 'Appetizers and sorbets and so on.'

13

'Strewth!' I said, with an involuntary shudder. The very idea of having to munch my way through 55 separate courses made me feel positively unwell. 'Did Mrs Pinchbeck say what the problem was?'

I took off my Wellington boots and found a pair of more respectable shoes which weren't coated with mud. As I did so, I remembered that there had been a narrowly averted disaster at the Pinchbecks' home a short time earlier. Guests at a children's party the Pinchbecks had organised, had found some giant hogweed stems and turned them into peashooters. Quite a number of the children had suffered severe allergy reactions. Fortunately, none of them had died.

'She said she thought that one of their guests might have developed some sort of allergy,' said Patsy. She didn't seem to think it was terribly urgent but I said I thought you'd want to go now. I'll keep lunch until you get back.'

'They seem prone to allergy problems down at the Pinchbecks!' I said, still thinking of the children's party that had gone wrong. 'What are we having for lunch?'

'Cheese and onion rolls with pickled gherkins on the side. Followed by a banana au naturelle and a cup of something made from hot water and ground Arabica beans.'

'That sounds like four courses.'

'If you have a chocolate from that box Frank and Gilly gave us for our anniversary then it'll be a five course meal.'

'Marvellous!'

I kissed my wife, picked up my black medical bag from my consulting room and set off for the Pinchbecks'. I was still wearing my gardening clothes but I had at least changed my shoes.

A few minutes later, I drove into the driveway of the Pinchbecks' house. Since I'd been there last, they had extended the driveway and laid down an expanded and generous version of one of those large circular, gravel areas which enable visitors to drive around a centre point. In this case the centre point was, as is so often the case, a large old-fashioned fountain. This one was well equipped with nymphs and cherubs and fish. Sadly, none of them was spouting water. Either the water had not yet been connected to the fountain or the Pinchbecks hadn't turned on the pumps required to make the fountain work. Few things seem sadder or more pointless than a fountain with no water coming out of it – especially if the fountain has been well equipped with potential water squirting sites. The cherubs and nymphs and so on, all designed and poised to spout water, now looked merely sad and redundant. Maybe the Pinchbecks liked it that way.

Mrs Pinchbeck met me at the door and took me into the dining room where her husband and her guests were all busily working their way through their next course. Dirty dishes and cutlery were piled high on the sideboard and through an open doorway, I could see into the kitchen where a young man, presumably Eric Harrison, was bent over the sink. He had a pink, frilly edged pinafore tied around his waist. I didn't envy him and hoped the Pinchbecks were paying him well for 12 hours of washing up. From the pile of dirty dishes stacked and waiting their turn, it was pretty clear that he was going to have his work cut out to keep up with the rate at which crockery was being used. A pleasantly plump, middle-aged woman in a white uniform was dashing about with steaming pans of something. She, I assumed, was Eric's mum.

The patient was Topham Beauclerk, the bookseller.

He was sitting at the table with the other guests. They were all busily munching their way through what looked like small sausage rolls which were swimming in a rich, red sauce of some kind.

'Shall we go somewhere a little more private?' I asked him.

'No, no, I'm fine sitting here,' said Mr Beauclerk. 'I seem to have developed some sort of allergy. Can you give me an antihistamine or something?'

He pulled back his right shirt sleeve and showed me his right forearm. There was a red allergy rash clearly visible. He wheezed a little as he spoke.

'Where else is the rash?' I asked him.

'Pretty well everywhere,' he replied. He put a forkful of sausage roll into his mouth and chewed at it noisily.

I thought him rather an odd and unpleasant fellow; packed to the gills with oodles of self-esteem, far more than was necessary, good for him or quite polite.

'Do you always have a wheeze?'

'Good God, no!' he said, without bothering to stop chewing. 'I assumed it was part of this damned allergy thing.'

'It probably is. Do you have any other symptoms?'

'I've been sneezing a bit. And I feel a trifle nauseous.'

15

'Do you have any difficulty in swallowing?'

'A little,' he admitted. 'My throat may be swollen slightly.'

'Do you have any known allergies? Any food allergies?'

He said he hadn't.

I asked him what he had eaten that might have caused his symptoms. He said he couldn't remember what he'd eaten and that it was surely my job to decide what had caused his symptoms. As he spoke, he sprayed food around. He didn't seem to care about this, or to be embarrassed.

Mr Pinchbeck, looking rather embarrassed by his guest's rudeness, and coming to my help, said they had all eaten smoked salmon and scrambled eggs. It had been their third course. He mentioned this because he wondered if the fish might have been the cause of the problem.

I said I thought that the salmon was probably the culprit.

'Have you ever had anything like this before?' I asked.

His mouth was full so he shook his head. He seemed to be coping quite well with the nausea from which he claimed to be suffering.

'I'll give you an antihistamine injection,' I told him. 'But you'd better keep away from fish in the future.'

'Just salmon you mean?'

'No, you need to avoid all fish dishes. If you have an allergy to one type of fish it is perfectly possible that you will be allergic to other types of fish. And it's quite possible that you could develop an allergy reaction simply by being in the same room as fish being cooked.'

'Never had trouble with fish before,' said Mr Beauclerk, as though this made it impossible that he should have trouble with it now. 'And I do a little fishing myself,' he added inconsequentially. 'Fly fishing, don't you know.'

I turned to Mrs Pinchbeck. 'Do you have any other fish courses planned?'

She consulted a well-thumbed sheet which she took from a pocket in her skirt. It was clearly the menu for their seemingly never-ending feast. 'We have smoked herrings as course no 11 and trout with almonds as number 24.' She showed me the menu. Just looking at the list of dishes they had planned made me feel queasy. I had a powerful feeling that it would be something of a miracle if the diners all managed to get to the end of their feast. Why, I couldn't help

16

wondering, didn't Mr Pinchbeck celebrate his birthday by taking his chums along to the Duck and Puddle to enjoy one of Gilly's steak and kidney pies. They could, if they'd had any room left, follow it up with a slice of treacle tart or a helping of spotted dick with plenty of custard.

'You mustn't eat those courses,' I told Mr Beauclerk. 'And while those dishes are being cooked, prepared and served you must keep out of the kitchen and the dining room.'

'Absurd!' said Mr Beauclerk. 'I've never had any problem with fish until you came along.' He said this as though as I were the cause of his symptoms. He swallowed. 'And why do I have to keep out of the way when fish is being cooked? Are you worried that the fish might jump out of the dish and nibble my nose? Do you think it is going to leap off the plate and bite me?' He laughed and looked around the table. There were some titters and a guffaw from his fellow guests.

'Well, I'm afraid I think you probably have a fish allergy now,' I told him. I really didn't much care for this fellow. 'And if you are allergic to fish and you eat it again then there is a chance that you could have a full-blooded anaphylactic shock reaction. You also need to avoid vapour produced when fish is being cooked because that could produce a reaction.'

'What does that mean, in English?' he demanded, his rudeness growing.

'It means there is a chance you could die if you ignore what I'm telling you,' I said.

'Oh, well, we're all going to die eventually!' said Mr Beauclerk, with a wave of his hands. 'You're not frightening me that easily.'

'I'm not trying to frighten you,' I told him firmly. 'I'm merely warning you what might happen if you aren't careful.' I was tempted to tell him that I really didn't give a damn whether he listened to my advice or not.

Mr Beauclerk refused to leave the dining room for me to give him an injection. Instead, he stood up and lowered his trousers and told me to swab the skin and jab the needle into his thigh while everyone else carried on eating.

Giving in to his stubbornness, I opened my black bag and took out a syringe and a vial of an antihistamine. Suddenly, he pulled up his trousers and sat down again. 'I don't feel as bad as I did,' he said abruptly. 'The incident has passed.'

It was true that the rash seemed to be fading and the wheezing was nowhere near as bad as it had been. 'I still think I should give you an injection,' I said. 'Or at the very least you should let me give you a couple of antihistamine tablets.'

'No, no, no!' he said, waving a hand imperiously. 'On your way, doctor! My body has healed itself. Your services are no longer required.' He then laughed loudly. He seemed to be playing to his audience and they responded with more titters and, I have to say, some rather uncomfortable laughter. The Pinchbecks both looked deeply embarrassed.

Under the circumstances there was nothing else I could do. I could hardly force the man to allow me to treat him. I said goodbye to everyone and drove back home to have my lunch. I was looking forward to my cheese and onion rolls and my coffee. And then, with a little luck, I was hoping that I could get back to my bonfire.

But my luck was out.

Just as I finished the last of my coffee, the telephone rang. It had, at least, had the decency to wait until I'd finished my lunch.

It was Mrs Pinchbeck again. She sounded panicky.

'You must come quickly, doctor!' she shouted. 'It's an emergency.'

'What's happened?' I asked.

'It's Mr Beauclerk,' she said.

'Did he eat more fish?'

'He insisted on eating the herrings.'

'And what's happened?'

'He's having difficulty breathing. His face is all swollen.'

'Lie him down, on his side and make sure his airway is open.'

'My husband has done all that. He went on a first aid course at the bank.'

'Good. I'm on my way. And I'll ask my wife to call an ambulance.'

I put down the telephone receiver, asked Patsy to ring for an ambulance to go to the Pinchbecks' address, picked up my black bag and was in the car and on my way within a minute and a half of receiving the call.

18

Life is a constant near death experience but Mr Beauclerk was frighteningly close to taking the final curtain when I arrived at the Pinchbecks'.

He had suffered an anaphylactic shock reaction and the ferryman was preparing to take him on that final journey across the Styx. He was still breathing, but with considerable difficulty; his heart was still beating, but hardly healthily; and when I checked his blood pressure, I found it had collapsed.

'We told him he shouldn't have eaten any more fish,' said one of the other guests. I didn't notice which one it was.

'He wouldn't listen,' said Mrs Pinchbeck who was close to tears.

I took out a syringe, a needle and a glass vial of adrenalin. I broke the top off the vial, filled the syringe with adrenalin and squirted the stuff into the foolish dinner guest.

Gradually, the adrenalin did its work. Mr Beauclerk began to breathe a little more easily, his blood pressure rose a little and his colour began to return.

'He'll need to go into the hospital in Barnstaple,' I told Mr Pinchbeck, who was kneeling beside me.

'Could he have a relapse?'

'I hope not. But he needs to be in hospital for a few days just in case.' I took some notepaper out of my bag and wrote an explanatory note for the hospital doctor who would have to admit Mr Beauclerk. I put the note into an envelope.

The ambulance arrived twenty minutes or so later. The driver had done well since they'd had to come from Barnstaple. The journey from the ambulance station to the Pinchbecks' home is only about 11 miles but it's a difficult 11 miles; all twists and turns and bad bends.

By the time the ambulance had arrived, Mr Beauclerk had more or less recovered and naturally, though he felt and looked weak, he didn't want to go to hospital.

'You're going,' I told him firmly, feeling that this was not the time for arguments or discussions.

'You can't make me,' he said, defiantly. He tried to get up but he was as weak as the proverbial kitten and he fell back down again immediately.

'I think Mr Beauclerk is a little confused,' I told one of the ambulance men. 'He definitely needs to be in hospital.' I handed over the envelope containing the note I had written.

19

'No problem, doctor,' said the ambulance man. He slipped the envelope into his jacket pocket. The two of them lifted a protesting Mr Beauclerk onto a stretcher, wrapped a blanket around him and fastened him to the stretcher with straps.

Mr Beauclerk tried to lift himself up but failed. 'Maybe you're right, doctor,' he said, when he found he was unable to move. 'I do seem to be rather weak.' I don't think he realised he was strapped to the stretcher. He turned his head. 'I'll want a refund of part of my £20,' he said, not addressing anyone in particular but clearly speaking to the Pinchbecks. 'And I'll pick up the bottles of wine I brought with me when I'm feeling better.'

The ambulance men took him away.

I don't think anyone was sorry to see him go.

I put the used syringe, together with the needle and the remains of the glass vial into my bag, locked it and said goodbye to the Pinchbecks and their other guests. And as the ambulance roared off to Barnstaple, bells ringing and lights flashing, I headed steadily back to Bilbury Grange.

I thought I might treat myself to a second cup of coffee before I lit my bonfire. I had, it seemed, been looking forward to that bonfire for a week. It was difficult to believe I had only built it a few hours ago.

I had restocked my bag and finished the coffee and was reflecting on how fortunate I was that Patsy had no more affection for dinner parties than I did, when the telephone rang again. Some days are like that. It was, by now, about three o'clock in the afternoon.

This time it was Mr Pinchbeck, rather than his wife, on the other end of the telephone.

'I'm so sorry to bother you again, doctor,' he said, sounding genuinely apologetic. 'But we're having a problem with another of our guests.'

'What seems to be the problem?' I asked, doing my best to hide my weariness and resorting to a favourite medical cliché. With the amount of food being consumed at the Pinchbecks', I half expected to be told that the entire dinner party cast had collapsed with digestive upsets. If I had eaten a quarter of the meal they had planned, it would have been me, not the table, which would have been groaning.

'It's Constance Chatterton' said Mr Pinchbeck. 'She's having a bit of a funny turn.'

'What sort of funny turn? What symptoms? Do I need to call an ambulance for her?'

'Oh no, I don't think she'll need an ambulance,' said Mr Pinchbeck. 'Indeed, I sincerely hope not.'

I told him I'd be there as quickly as I could. Once again, I said goodbye to Patsy, told her where I was going, picked up my black bag and headed for the car. If the Rolls had been a horse it would have doubtless found its way to the Pinchbecks' without any help from me.

Mrs Chatterton was still sitting at the Pinchbecks' dining table. The other guests had not stopped eating but Mrs Chatterton seemed to be taking a breather.

'What's the problem?' I asked her, more breezily than I felt.

'My vision is blurred,' said Mrs Chatterton. 'And I've got an itchy rash.' She was slurring her words and it was clear that she had been drinking. I wasn't surprised to hear that she had been drinking. The guests would definitely need a good deal of fluid to help wash down all that food.

'Where is the itchy rash?'

'Pretty well everywhere.'

'Is there anything else?'

'I don't think so.'

'Did the symptoms come on suddenly or slowly?'

'Rather slowly.'

'Do you have any food allergies that you know of?'

'No, no I don't think so.'

'What have you had to drink?'

'Just a couple of gin and tonics. I don't drink wine. I'm not terribly keen on it.'

'How many gin and tonics?'

'Two or three,' she replied.

'Seven or eight,' whispered her husband. 'But they were very weak. They contained far more tonic than gin.'

'Are you sure there aren't any other symptoms?' I asked her.

She frowned, thinking hard. 'I don't think so,' she said.

'You said you had a ringing in your ears,' her husband reminded her.

21

'Oh yes. I forgot that. I have a ringing noise in my ears.'

And it was that which gave me the clue. I asked Mrs Pinchbeck to fetch one of the bottles of tonic water so that I could look at the label. And sure enough the tonic contained a fairly hefty quantity of quinine.

There had for some time been an on-going campaign to get a reduction in the amount of quinine in tonic water. But back in the 1970s, some brands of tonic water still contained an unhealthy quantity of the stuff.

'How many bottles of this has she drunk?' I asked Mrs Pinchbeck.

She went out into the kitchen to check on the collection of bottles which had accumulated.

'Seven,' she told me when she returned.

'Seven bottles of tonic water?'

'Yes.'

And then I was sure of the diagnosis.

'I think your problem is caused by the quinine in the tonic water,' I told Mrs Chatterton. 'It happens sometimes. And your symptoms are fairly classic ones.

She laughed. It was a strange, almost hysterical sort of laugh. 'Not the gin, then?'

'No, not the gin.'

'I should have had more gin and less tonic water.'

'That would have caused a different set of problems.'

'I suppose so.'

'What's the treatment?' asked Mr Chatterton. 'Can you give her anything?'

'I'm afraid I'm going to have to send her to hospital,' I told him.

The Pinchbecks' dinner party was beginning to resemble their children's party which had resulted in most of the guests ending up as patients in the local hospital.

'Is that really necessary?' asked Mr Chatterton.

'I'm afraid so,' I told him. 'I'm sure she'll be fine but I want them to do some tests and keep an eye on her for a day or two.'

'We'll soon have to move what remains of our dinner party to the hospital!' said Mr Balfour Morrison, the school-teacher and broadcaster. He seemed to think this was funny. 'Still, there's more food for those of us still here, eh?'

The Pinchbecks both looked at him. Mr Morrison seemed unaware that the sick woman's husband was not two yards away from him. If anyone had spoken like that when Patsy was being sent into hospital, I would have been unable to resist the temptation to see whether my fist was made of sterner stuff than his nose.

The appalling Morrison grinned and raised a wine glass in a callous salute. I really wasn't terribly impressed by the Pinchbecks' choice of friends.

'Have you got a phone I could use?' I asked Mr Pinchbeck.

He showed me into a tiny room which he used as a study. It was barely big enough for a desk and a chair but there was a telephone on the desk.

I shut the door and rang for an ambulance. When I'd done that there was time for me to ring the hospital in Barnstaple.

I explained the situation to the young doctor to whom I spoke. It turned out that he was the doctor who had admitted Mr Beauclerk. He sounded astonished that he was about to receive another guest from the same dinner party.

'How many more people have you got there?' he asked.

'Just five more to go,' I told him.

'Some dinner party! Try not to send them all in,' he said. 'We're getting a bit tight on beds.'

I said I would do my best then I hung up and went back out into the dining room.

Mrs Chatterton was comfortable enough and clearly not deteriorating. The damage had been done but it would not, I was sure, leave any permanent damage.

I left the Pinchbecks' before the ambulance arrived and then I headed back to Bilbury Grange. As I left, Mrs Harrison was serving another course and her son was still washing dishes. The Pinchbecks had clearly decided to continue with their decimated dinner party. The show must go on. I heard someone say it was course 42. I didn't stop to find out what the course consisted of as it was nearly time for my dinner.

I had just about finished my evening meal, a chunky slice of home-made vegetarian pizza accompanied by a very refreshing glass of home-made lemonade, when I received the next call from the Pinchbecks. Somehow, it wasn't a complete surprise. When a group of people eat so much food and drink, and wash it down with so

23

much alcohol, there are almost certain to be problems. The human body isn't built for 55 course meals.

This time, it was Mr Pinchbeck who telephoned. I wondered if he and his wife were now drawing lots to see who made the call.

'I feel so embarrassed to be ringing you again,' he said.

And, to be fair, he did sound embarrassed.

Actually, I felt embarrassed for him. How many patients have had to call their doctor four times in a single day?

Job had his boils to deal with. Dante had the nine circles of hell to pass through. And now I had the Pinchbecks' dinner party. Sorting out their darned dinner party guests was beginning to feel like my life's work. I began to sympathise with that bloke Sisyphus, the chap who was forever pushing a boulder up a hill. Actually, the way things were going, I seemed to be forever pushing the wrong damned boulder up the wrong damned hill.

'One of our guests has been shot,' said Mr Pinchbeck.

I could hardly believe it.

Sometimes, things just go one way. The lucky gambler has a surprising streak of luck. The businessman has a run of bad luck. You can't manage these things: they just happen.

'I'm on my way,' I told him. 'Do I need to ring for an ambulance? Do you need to call the police?'

'I think we probably need both,' he said. 'Actually, two of our guests have been shot. Both Balfour Morrison and Elmore Chatterton have been shot in the leg.'

'Have you controlled the bleeding?'

'Yes, more or less.'

'Who shot them?'

'Our Labrador puppy.'

'Your Labrador puppy shot both Balfour Morrison and Elmore Chatterton?'

'Yes.'

The day was becoming stranger by the minute.

'Whose gun was it?'

'Elmore Chatterton's.'

'I'll be there as soon as I can,' I told him. I wondered if the dog had shot the two men separately or if he'd shot them both with a single blast of the gun. The latter seemed more likely. It was difficult to imagine the Pinchbecks' playful Labrador puppy having some sort of brainstorm and going on a wild shooting rampage. But the way the day was going, I wouldn't have regarded that as impossible. 'I'll ask Patsy to telephone for an ambulance,' I told Mr Pinchbeck. 'I'll leave you to telephone the police if you think they should be there.'

'You won't be ringing the police?'

'I need to get into the car and get down there as soon as I can. I'll leave calling them to you.'

To be honest, I'm a bit old-fashioned and I don't think it is a doctor's job to call the police if a patient is injured.

Once again, I asked Patsy to send an ambulance to the Pinchbecks' and then I put my black bag back into the car.

I really felt that by now the Rolls probably could find its way down to the Pinchbecks' house without my help. We slid into the Pinchbecks' driveway and it felt strangely like coming home.

It turned out that Mr Morrison and Mr Chatterton had been shot in the calf while sitting at the table.

The remaining diners had taken their statutory 30-minute break from eating, and Mr Chatterton had gone outside to shoot some birds. He'd wandered around outside for twenty minutes or so, firing into the woods where he thought he'd seen a few crows and pigeons, and when he had come back into the house he had left his shotgun leaning against a chair. He said he thought that the gun was unloaded. Tragically, it wasn't. The Pinchbecks' dog brushed against the gun, knocking it over, and then, as it stumbled, the poor beast trod on the trigger. The pellets had scattered across quite a large area but miraculously the only victims had been Mr Morrison and Mr Chatterton himself. Surprisingly, it is not at all unusual for people to be shot with their own guns, with the trigger having being pressed by a dog. I wondered if Mr Pinchbeck had called the police. I wondered whether they would decide to arrest the poor dog. Actually, I couldn't help wondering whether I'd been told the whole story. Mr Chatterton seemed to me to be a pretty unpleasant character. Maybe one of the other guests had fired the gun and hit Mr Morrison by accident. Maybe someone had shot them both. There was no butler available as a possible suspect but there was always Eric Harrison. Maybe a day spent washing interminable dishes in the Pinchbecks' kitchen had deranged him.

I decided it was nothing to do with me and I didn't really care terribly much if he had shot them both so I dismissed all these strange thoughts. The day was strange enough as it was. And I was rapidly losing sympathy with this unpleasant bunch of bezzlers.

There were quite a few pellets embedded in Mr Harrison's calf and the pellets were huge. From what I could see they looked as if they were made of lead. They were the size of small marbles. Mrs Pinchbeck was holding his leg in an attempt to staunch the bleeding. Unfortunately, she wasn't making a terribly good job of it. Blood was still pouring out from the wounds the pellets had made and from the position of the wounds, I hazarded a guess that the posterior tibial artery had been damaged. Mr Harrison was moaning; partly in pain and partly, I suspected, as a result of the shock. When you are sitting at a dinner table working your way through a 55-item menu, you may reasonably expect to find yourself coping with indigestion, heartburn and an attack of wind but you probably don't expect to be hit by some chunky sized lead pellets fired from a fellow diner's resting, and seemingly harmless, shotgun.

'Press harder on the wound,' I told Mrs Pinchbeck.

With some obvious reluctance, she did as I had asked.

When I was satisfied that the bleeding had been staunched, I left Mr Harrison while I took a look at Mr Chatterton's injury.

Mr Chatterton's injury wasn't as bad because he had been hit by just two or three pellets. But he too was bleeding badly. A smallish artery, probably the peroneal or fibular artery, a subsidiary branch of the posterior tibial artery, had been severed and blood was pumping out at quite a rate. It was some time since I'd studied anatomy but it's amazing how these bits and pieces of information drift back into the conscious mind when they are needed and appropriate.

Mr Chatterton was attempting to stop the bleeding by pressing on it but he wasn't pressing hard enough. Unlike venous blood, which just trickles out, arterial blood comes out of the vessel under pressure and can spurt feet or even yards into the air. The spray of blood from both legs made it quite clear that both Mr Harrison and Mr Chatterton had suffered significant arterial damage. It was, I thought, a good thing that I had managed to get to the Pinchbecks' without much delay. And it was a good thing that I had asked Patsy to call for an ambulance.

GPs don't usually find themselves treating more than one patient at a time. When it happens, you have to use the triage system utilised in military hospitals such as American MASH units. The patient who is most seriously wounded must be treated as a priority, though you do what you can to stabilise the less seriously wounded.

It seemed pretty clear that Mr Chatterton's injury was less serious than Mr Harrison's. But he seemed to be losing more blood than Mr Harrison. It seemed clear that the arterial damage to Mr Chatterton's leg was more severe than the damage to Mr Harrison's leg. They were both going to need surgery but my job was clearly simply to limit the loss of blood and keep both men alive until they could be taken to the hospital.

'Do you have something I can use as a tourniquet?' I asked Mrs Harrison, who had stopped cooking to watch the excitement.

'What sort of thing?' she asked.

'Something I can tie around Mr Chatterton's leg.'

'I don't think you should put on a tourniquet,' said someone. I looked up. Mr Pinchbeck was standing over me. 'Our first aid teacher taught us that tourniquets can be dangerous. He said that simply putting pressure on the site of the wound can be safer.'

'Sometimes,' I agreed. I wondered why Mr Pinchbeck, who looked very pale, wasn't doing something useful instead of merely offering theoretical advice.

It is true that tourniquets can be problematical if they are left on for too long but when you have two patients who are bleeding badly, it is vital to stop the flow of blood. And since I only had one pair of hands, and none of the others present seemed prepared or able to staunch the flow of blood, a tourniquet seemed to me to be the only solution. In fact, a tourniquet is only really a problem if it is left on for too long and the tissues are deprived of essential oxygen. If the tourniquet is loosened every few minutes, to allow blood to flow into the tissues, then no damage will be done.

'Excuse me,' I said to Mr Chatterton, 'do you mind if I use your tie to stop your bleeding?'

Mr Chatterton looked at me, then at his tie. It was a hideous thing in blue and orange. He shook his head. I unfastened the tie and then tied it around his thigh with a good knot so that I could unfasten it easily and quickly.

'I really, really don't think you should do that,' said Mr Pinchbeck.

'The alternative is to let the poor fellow bleed to death,' I pointed out, speaking softly so that only Mr Pinchbeck could hear me. There

27

was already a large puddle of blood on the floor. It is always difficult to estimate how much blood has been lost from a wound but I thought that Mr Chatterton had already lost at least half a pint of the good stuff. If we left his leg to bleed then he would be dangerously exsanguinated by the time the ambulance arrived.

'Have you got a watch?' I asked Mr Pinchbeck.

'Yes, of course.'

'Then please tell me when ten minutes have passed. I'll then unfasten the tourniquet and let some blood through.' I checked the wound. The flow of blood had slowed almost to a standstill.

Mr Pinchbeck nodded.

He was, I hoped, learning fast that there is sometimes a difference between what makes sense in the classroom and what makes sense in a real emergency situation.

Once I'd tied a tourniquet round Mr Chatterton's leg, I went back to Mr Harrison. I had thought that I might be able to move at least one of the pellets but I decided not to move anything. There seemed a good chance that the pellet I could reach most easily was compressing a small blood vessel. If I moved it then there was a real chance that the bleeding would intensify. And Mr Harrison, like his fellow dinner party guest, had already lost a good deal of blood.

Thanking the sartorial gods that both men had been wearing ties, I obtained Mr Harrison's permission to remove his tie from around his neck and used it to tie a tourniquet above his knee. His tie was just as hideous as that belonging to Mr Chatterton. It was yellow and had little blue squares on it. I wonder who designs these things. Do they do it as a joke, perhaps?

Once the tourniquet was in place, the blood flow slowed to a trickle and then stopped.

Mr Harrison was enormous and his leg as thick as a telegraph pole. The tie was only just long enough.

He told me that he weighed a sixth of a ton and he seemed quite proud of this. The other man who had been shot, Mr Chatterton, later also boasted that he weighed several hundredweight. They both seemed proud to be indecently obese.

The particular act of eating is, like most human experiences, a transient experience. Sleeping, washing, listening to good music, sex, looking at good art – all these things are as transient as the enjoyment of good food, well prepared and served with panache.

28

But the consequences of eating are not transient and these two men were proof of that fact. Their weight had, I suspected, been rising steadily for the last 40 odd years.

'Will this do?' asked Mrs Harrison, holding out a tea towel. She was presumably offering it for use as a tourniquet. It was, of course, quite useless for that purpose.

'It's OK,' I told her, as kindly as I could manage. 'We've got what we need.'

'Am I going to die?' Mr Harrison asked.

'Not from this,' I replied.

I told both men that they would have to go to the Barnstaple casualty department so that the pellets could be removed safely and the damaged arteries stitched up. I reassured them both that although their injuries looked bad neither of them was in any serious danger.

'Will they be able to save my leg?' asked Mr Harrison.

I assured both men that there was no danger of either of them losing a limb.

'How did the gun come to be loaded?' I asked Mr Pinchbeck.

'Mr Chatterton had been out shooting,' he replied. 'We were taking one of our 30 minute breaks and he'd gone outside to see if he could find some birds to shoot.'

'Where was he shooting?' I asked.

'In the fields just beyond the end of our garden,' replied Mr Pinchbeck. 'And in the woodlands just over the fence. He was just having a bit of fun. Shooting a few birds.'

I find it difficult to understand why anyone would shoot wild birds for no reason other than that they are there – especially when those birds are no threat to him or his crops and are not going to be eaten or used in any way. What sort of person kills animals just for fun?

'Have you got permission for your guests to shoot in there?' I asked him.

I was furious that he would think it 'fun' for one of his guests to wander around the countryside shooting birds for absolutely no reason other than the fact that he could.

'No,' said Mr Pinchbeck, rather defiantly. 'Am I supposed to get permission before allowing my guests to shoot in the countryside?'

'Of course you are! All sorts of people walk in those woods. Children play in the woods. Ramblers and hikers walk in them.'

'I didn't know that. How was I supposed to know?'

'You could have asked someone,' I said.

'Well, it didn't occur to me.'

'Let's hope no one was hit by a stray shot,' I said.

I suddenly realised that I was interrogating Mr Pinchbeck like a policeman. In addition to the fact that his guest had been shooting birds for 'fun', I was angry because I knew he could have easily hit an innocent rambler or a dog walker or a child. Or even a poacher passing through in search of game for food. I realised that it wasn't my place to decide whether or not he had been behaving badly. I shut up and walked away.

The gunman seemed to me to have all the moral character, and sense of responsibility, one might reasonably associate with the sort of creatures you find when you lift a small rock in the garden.

'What's the time? Is the ten minutes up?' I asked him.

Mr Pinchbeck looked at his watch. 'Oh, yes. Just about.'

I released both tourniquets and let some blood into the tissues. After a minute or so, I retied the tourniquets.

While I waited for the ambulance to arrive, I rang the hospital and spoke to the young doctor on call. He actually laughed when I told him I was sending two more of the Pinchbecks' dinner guests to the hospital. 'They've both been shot,' I told him. 'You'll have to dig out some lead shot but they aren't too seriously injured.'

'It sounds to me as though you've wandered into an Agatha Christie novel!' he said. 'The last one standing will be the guilty one.'

The ambulance crew were the same pair who had taken Mr Beauclark to the hospital. 'Shall we just come back here when we've delivered this pair?' asked the driver.

I felt sorry for the two of them, having to lift such obese creatures into the back of their ambulance.

'I hope the springs will cope,' said the driver, after he'd closed the back doors.

I hoped so too. I told them I sincerely hoped they wouldn't be needed again. I also told them about the tourniquets and the guy who was going to travel in the back of the ambulance promised to keep an eye on things and to unfasten the ties every few minutes.

When I left the Pinchbecks', a very weary Mrs Harrison was serving item no 55 on Mrs Pinchbeck's absurd menu. It had seemed absurd when they'd started the meal but now, for some reason, it seemed even more absurd, self-indulgent and utterly pointless.

Miraculously, Mrs Harrison still had a genuine and jolly smile on her face though the dinner party now seemed to me to be a rather sad affair. Most of the blood had been mopped up but the dining room still looked as though a battle had been fought there. Blood, especially when squirting out of damaged arteries, tends to travel quite a distance and just before I left I noticed that some had reached a picture hanging on the wall.

I got the impression that the two remaining guests and the Pinchbecks were now simply going through the motions of enjoying themselves. Why they didn't abandon their ill-fated dinner party was quite beyond me. The only people left at the dining table were Claude Templeton and the two Pinchbecks. I could only imagine that they were all suffering from shock and were carrying on without really realising what they were doing.

If you looked around and didn't realise that there should have been five guests you'd have thought that everything was really quite normal. Mrs Harrison's son, young Eric, was still washing dishes and his equally long-suffering mum was still cooking and serving.

I felt sorry for the Harrisons. They were hard workers. I wondered if Mrs Pinchbeck had thought to offer them anything to eat or drink.

As I drove slowly home I realised there had been no sign of the police at the Pinchbecks. I wondered if they realised that the hospital would have to call the police. No hospital doctor can treat a gun wound without informing the authorities. I supposed that I should have advised the Pinchbecks to leave the gun where it had fallen – and not touch it. But I had been rather too busy dealing with the wounded to worry about the cause of their injuries. The Labrador who had inadvertently fired the gun had been nowhere to be seen.

Back home I parked the car in the driveway and sniffed the now cool evening air.

I could smell smoke.

I could definitely smell smoke.

I hurried into the house and found Patsy. I didn't have to ask her what was burning. From the kitchen window, I could see a curl of smoke rising at the bottom of the garden.

'My bonfire!' I cried. 'What's happened to it?'

31

'I'm so sorry,' said Patsy, who looked and sounded genuinely upset for she knew how much I'd been looking forward to lighting my bonfire. 'Mr Parfitt happened to it.'

Mr Parfitt is our gardener. He has been helping me look after our garden for years. But he has one, singular weakness: he does not understand my penchant for garden bonfires. He sometimes pretends to understand and share my passion for lighting fires. But deep down I know he has never properly understood.

'Mr Parfitt came by while you were out,' explained Patsy. 'He said he had to do something in the greenhouse.'

'But while he was here...'

'Exactly! As he left, he said he'd lit the bonfire for you. He said he thought it was likely to rain later on and that if you were delayed you might have difficulty lighting the fire.' Patsy touched my arm. 'I'm sorry, my love.'

I looked out silently at the plume of smoke. It had clearly been a very good bonfire. Unbeknownst to Mr Parfitt, there was so much paper packed underneath a weatherproof cover of old branches that it would not have been difficult to light even if it had been pouring with rain.

'I'll just wander down the garden and take a look at it,' I said to Patsy. 'Make sure everything is OK.'

'It'll be chilly in an hour or so,' said Patsy, who knew that I would be disappointed by the fact that my putative bonfire was now just a pile of smoking ash. And she certainly knew that I'd had a long and arduous day dealing with the Pinchbecks' party guests. 'So I've laid a fire in the drawing room.' She smiled at me. 'Perhaps you'd light it when you come in?'

Patsy can light a fire just as well as I can, of course.

A fire in the living room hearth wasn't quite the same as an enormous bonfire. But it would make an excellent substitute.

'They're showing *The Thirty Nine Steps* on the television,' continued Patsy. 'The Hitchcock version with Robert Donat and Madeleine Carroll. And afterwards, they're showing the 1938 Hitchcock version of *The Lady Vanishes*; the one with Margaret Lockwood and Michael Redgrave and May Whitty as Miss Froy. We could watch them both, if you like. And you could make some toast. Use the brass toasting fork and toast the bread in front of the fire.'

I perked up noticeably. *The Thirty Nine Steps* is one of my favourite films. And I love Basil Radford and Naunton Wayne as Charters and Caldicott in *The Lady Vanishes*. And with most of the Pinchbecks' dinner guests already in hospital there was a good chance I would be able to watch both films all the way through. Hot buttered toast, made with a toasting fork in front of a blazing log fire, would be a huge and welcome bonus. Toast never tastes as good as it does when it has been made in front of a log fire.

Belatedly, and with some shame, I noticed for the first time that while I'd been out, Patsy had changed into one of her prettiest and most alluring frocks. There was just a promising hint of cleavage. She'd done something to her hair too. And I could smell the enticing smell of an expensive perfume which Gilly had bought Patsy for her birthday.

'You look very beautiful!' I told her.

And then we kissed.

'You've had a long day,' she said, a few minutes later. 'I'll open that new bottle of malt whisky, and put it with a glass by your chair.'

A beautiful wife. A log fire. A couple of favourite movies. A comfortable, old armchair and a glass or two of something good.

Heaven takes many forms.

I called to Ben, our faithful dog, and together we tottered down the garden to check on the remains of the bonfire, and to sniff the slightly smoky evening air.

And after that there was still a great deal to look forward to.

For the Pinchbecks, a strange and painful day was doubtless coming to a close.

But at Bilbury Grange, the best part of the day was yet to come.

The Poacher: A Man of Quiet Integrity

I knew him from the Duck and Puddle.

He supplied Frank and Gilly, the landlord and landlady of the Bilbury village pub, with a steady supply of rabbits, pheasant and trout. Unlike Mr Chatterton, the Pinchbecks' guest, he never shot or caught anything which wasn't going to be eaten. Frank and Gilly paid him with whisky and sandwiches and with essential provisions such as salt, cheese and a loaf of bread. I'm pretty sure that no money ever changed hands. Toby was not a man for whom money meant a great deal, though he would occasionally get paid in cash when doing odd jobs for local farmers and landowners.

Toby was a patient of mine, by which I mean only that he lived in the village of Bilbury and since there were no other doctors in the area, he was registered as a patient of mine. But he had never once been to the surgery, or asked me to visit him at home. If he had a problem, any sort of problem, he dealt with it himself. He was someone who took the phrase 'self-sufficiency' very seriously. It was the way he lived his life.

Lots of people play at self-sufficiency. Town folk go out into the woods to pick mushrooms and berries and end up picking stuff that makes them ill. My friend Will, who practises as a doctor in a town practice, told me that he has a patient who has a hazelnut bush in his garden and who rushes out and digs up nuts he has seen the squirrels burying. Will also has a patient who keeps a pig in his compact, suburban, back garden and who spends much of his life repairing fences, both literally and figuratively. Will says that he is sure that these folk mean well and that they think that keeping half a dozen hens or a couple of geese means that they are living the good life. In truth, of course, they are merely playing at simplicity and self-sufficiency. Toby was living it.

I had known Toby for years. He always looks rather worn out, and reminded me of an old car which has never been repaired, restored or fussed over. An old car may have a few dings in the bodywork and some cracks in the leather seats. But it still does what is expected of it.

Winter or summer, he wore an old waxed raincoat over a thick jacket and a pair of corduroy trousers. If it wasn't actually raining, the top few inches of a roll necked jumper could just be seen. The belt of the raincoat had long since disappeared and had, inevitably, I suppose, been replaced by a piece of dark blue baler twine. (He used blue rather than orange because it was less visible in the countryside.) Two more lengths of baler twine, also blue, were tied around the legs of his trousers, just above ankle height. When I asked him about these, he said they were there to stop snakes and vermin crawling up his trouser leg when he was lying in the woods or on a riverbank. He never removed the raincoat, and only rarely removed the old tweed cap which he wore rather rakishly to one side. Even when he was sitting in the snug at the Duck and Puddle, he still wore his outdoor coat. However, he had the manners of a gentleman and he always lifted the cap if a woman entered the room. His hair was thin, unkempt and grey and looked as if it had been cut by someone wielding a pair of scissors, possibly in front of the mirror and possibly without the aid of a reflection. I'm confident he always cut it himself. He wore fingerless, knitted gloves which were beginning to unravel.

Generally speaking, the only parts of him which were visible were his face and fingertips but these told the story of a man who has lived his life out of doors, and had never fussed with moisturising cream. Surprisingly, perhaps, he was clean-shaven, though he did sport a pair of rather extravagantly bushy sideburns.

His eyelids were red rimmed with chronic blepharitis and both his conjunctiva red veined from constant exposure to the North Devon wind. His left eye had a ptosis. His skin was rough and his cheeks red veined from a mixture of wind and whisky. He had eyes which had seen a great deal. He was a quiet man who knew a good deal more than he told, unlike the noisy folk who tell more than they know.

Thumper, who revered him, said Toby knew everything there was to know about the countryside; he knew nothing that was not worth knowing and not worth learning.

Toby had hardly ever left Bilbury.

As a young man he had visited Exeter once; delivering a horse for a local farmer. Once the horse had been delivered, he had turned the horse box round and driven straight back. It had, I suspect, never occurred to him to stay and take a look at the city. His world was in Bilbury and the boundary of his world was probably the distance a man could walk from the Duck and Puddle in half a day. (Allowing the other half a day for the walk back.)

He owned just one book, an old family Bible, nearly six inches thick and fastened with a brass clasp which was fitted with a stout lock.

His one luxury was the *Sporting Life* newspaper which he collected every Saturday from Peter Marshall's village shop, though as far as anyone knew he never placed a bet. He paid for the newspaper, and any other essentials he occasionally purchased, with a freshly caught pheasant or rabbit. As with the Duck and Puddle, it was very rare for money to ever change hands.

From afar, Toby always seemed to be rather stern and sad and earnest. There was a strange mixture of innocence and worldliness about him and although it is probably an exaggeration to say that he was much loved, he was certainly admired and respected for his independence and his skills.

He was a religious man, a firm believer in a benevolent God who could, if the occasion warranted it, express a profound fury. He never went to church, however, and had probably never been in a church in his life. He would have been embarrassed to sit there in his raincoat, tied up with baler twine, alongside worshippers in their Sunday best.

His one weakness was that he took everything he heard at face value. He was an honest and straightforward man himself and tended to believe what he heard others say. He once sat in the Duck and Puddle and heard some tourists discussing religion. One of them, an obnoxious academic well-known to television viewers but unknown to Toby, loud-mouthed and arrogant and full of his own self-importance, stated that God did not exist, and made the statement with such force that it appeared that he had inside information confirming his belief. Toby was deeply depressed for a month afterwards. 'How did that man know the truth of what he said?' he asked Frank Parsons weeks later. Frank assured him that the visitor was, in his view, an unpleasant lunatic who existed only to shock and to startle and to disconcert and who had mistaken his television persona for his real one. Eventually, Toby accepted Frank's reassurance. But the man caused much unhappiness and I doubt very much if Toby was the first or last person to be so distressed by his unsupported, and unsupportable, allegations.

When he moved, Toby walked cautiously, in that way people walk on frost-hardened rutted earth or an ice slippery pavement. He wore well-worn and well-oiled boots and he could move without making a sound. He kept the leather greased so that it remained waterproof and never squeaked.

Quite a few people in the village were frightened of him though he was one of the gentlest and least threatening people I knew. Children used to keep out of his way and sometimes referred to him as the 'Bogeyman'. One villager once told me that his son, who was 22-years-old and a corporal in the British army, was still so terrified of the 'Bogeyman' that he wouldn't take the dog into the local woods in case they met.

Toby didn't smile often but when he did it was a revelation. It wasn't one of those 'celebrity smiles' which involve a lot of teeth but nothing in the eyes. His smile would take over his whole face. His eyes lit up and broad creases appeared around his mouth. For some reason he always smiled and nodded when he saw me. I felt strangely privileged.

Visitors who saw him tended to look down their noses, often mistaking him for a tramp or a beggar. He would gently but politely and firmly reject offers of food, drink or money. It was because he was a proud and independent man that he had chosen the life he lived.

I once asked Thumper, who knew him well, better than anyone in the village, how Toby had become a poacher.

I had, I think, entertained silly and romantic notions that he had perhaps run away from some city job, tired of the rat race. Had his wife left him? Had he lost his job or his driving licence and come to North Devon to forget, as a man might join the Foreign Legion?

Thumper laughed when I suggested these explanations; he explained that Toby had been an orphan, brought up by his grandparents. His mother had run away, no one could remember to where or for why, and his father, a farm labourer, had died in a tractor accident – a commoner countryside tragedy than most town

37

folk realise. His grandfather had been a poacher and had taught young Toby the trade, just as any man might pass on his valued skills to a youngster.

Toby's grandfather had, said Thumper, been quite a rogue. He had owned a mongrel dog which he had sold half a dozen times. On each occasion the dog had returned home immediately, finding his way home from Taunton, Exeter and, so Thumper swore, even from as far away as the village of Widecombe-in-the-Moor; the place which is famous as the home of Uncle Tom Cobleigh and all. The old man's dog had been trained so well that he could slip into a farmyard and bring a chicken out to the owner without disturbing the farmer or his dogs.

Toby had no dog but he kept a ferret in a capacious poacher's pocket which he had sewn into the inside of his waxed coat. Sometimes he carried the ferret in a trouser pocket. The ferret was rather old and, I suspect, kept more as a companion than as a hunting aide.

Poachers often keep ferrets for they are useful for hunting rabbits, as long as you don't over-feed them and let them get too fat and lazy. Some poachers put a muzzle on their ferret before putting it into a rabbit burrow, and some crueller ones will even sew up the ferret's lips so that it cannot eat or spoil the rabbit it catches. Some poachers starve their ferrets, to keep them keen, but Toby would never do that. And Toby had never muzzled his ferret in case the animal got lost in an extensive burrow. He explained to Thumper he couldn't bear the idea of a ferret of his dying of starvation because it was muzzled. He never sent a ferret down a hole with a collar on or a lead, either. He said that if you did this the ferret could get caught up in an underground root and die, alone, starving and in the darkness. If his ferret didn't emerge from a warren, Toby would put gorse into one rabbit hole and light it, smoking out the ferret and catching it as it left another hole. Rabbit burrows can sometimes be a maze of paths, linked to other burrows and threading through roots and other underground obstacles. A ferret, even an experienced one, can easily get lost when there may be over 100 yards of tunnel underground.

One evening in the Duck and Puddle, Thumper had told me that it had been Toby's grandfather who had taught him how to use his hands to tickle a trout out of a stream, how to make a simple snare to catch a rabbit, how to pick up a hedgehog without pricking yourself on the creature's spines and how to catch a hare with nothing more than two hands and an old coat.

It was Toby's grandfather who taught Thumper how to catch a pheasant with his bare hands (put the dregs from a whisky bottle onto some corn and lay the corn down on a path used by the pheasant, then put a sack over the pheasant when it becomes drunk).

And he taught him how to set a gate net for hares. (Throw a net over a five-barred gate leading out of a field in which a hare has been spotted. Put stones on the top of the gate to keep the net in place, then use bits of stone or gorse to block up all the holes in the stone wall which surrounds the field. Finally, walk across the field, with the hare ahead of you. The hare, finding its usual escape routes blocked, will head for the gate and get caught in the net.)

The old man, said Thumper, had been proud of his simple skills and happy to pass them on to a boy who wanted to learn.

'The single most important thing he taught me,' said Thumper, 'was that when you are walking in strange woods you should always look behind you every twenty yards or so, because what you see then will look different to what is in front of you. And when you make your way back out of the woods that will be the way you'll be looking.'

In a town I don't doubt that Toby would have been regarded as a fool; a silly old man with no knowledge or value. But Toby understood country ways better than anyone. He could use a knapped flint to light a bonfire in the rain and somehow it would smoke away merrily. He could forecast the weather better than any meteorologist and he could make a catapult or a bow with the makings he carried in his pocket.

There is no doubt that city folk, visiting Bilbury, frequently looked down on him, patronised him and regarded him as someone who was, in their terms, 'a loser'.

'He wouldn't last a minute in London,' I heard a visiting banker sneer. I think it was the blue baler twine around his raincoat and trousers which they couldn't quite understand.

It was probably true that Toby would have struggled to survive in London.

But would that banker and his posh pals have been able to go into the woods armed only with a penknife, a piece of string and a couple of knapped flints, and then catch a trout and a rabbit before building a wood fire and preparing a three course meal?

Somehow, I rather doubt it.

The key to survival anywhere is to live with the environment, to respect it, to understand it and to prepare and plan for the inevitable vicissitudes of the locality. The key to living comfortably is to understand the delights and the dangers, the advantages and the disadvantages; to be satisfied that you are where you want to be, and to adapt your lifestyle to the environment in which you have chosen to spend your years.

Toby, like my friends Thumper, Patchy, Frank and Peter, had adapted to his surroundings perfectly and he was entirely comfortable with the world in which he found himself when he woke each morning.

I wonder how many London bankers can say that about themselves.

Thumper told me that he once had a meal with Toby which consisted of poached trout served with freshly picked and sliced almonds, followed by rabbit cooked on a spit over a wood fire and served with wild sage and mushrooms. For pudding, Toby served a handful of wild strawberries and black raspberries.

Contrary to appearances, Toby was certainly no tramp and no beggar. He was a professional poacher and a proud one; it would have doubtless surprised many town dwellers to know that he was well tolerated by local landowners.

In some areas, poaching is a real nuisance, for greedy and unthinking poachers cause a great deal of damage and spoil the local hunting and fishing. Gangs of professional poachers come from towns and cities to collect game which they can sell to wholesalers. They arrive at night in trucks and four-wheeled drive vehicles, armed with guns and traps and nets and they indiscriminately take huge quantities of rabbits, hares, deer and pheasant. They catch geese, salmon and trout too. I've even heard of them taking swans. Worst of all, these city poachers cut through fences with wire cutters, they damage gates and then leave them open and they churn up fields with their vehicles. A proper countryman poacher, such as Toby, can travel through the countryside without leaving a trace of his passing but the gangs leave devastation behind them and are, understandably, loathed both by landowners and by poachers such as Toby who regard them as giving the trade a bad name.

But Bilbury was too far away from what some folk like to describe as civilisation for the poaching gangs to bother coming and local landowners had no trouble with them.

Toby, one of few professional poachers in North Devon, was accepted and even respected by the people from whose land he took what he needed. As he travelled around the local countryside, he mended broken fences and gates and layered hedges which were becoming thin and had developed gaps through which stock might wander. If a smallholder needed help then Toby would turn up, as if by magic, and spend a day digging or layering a hedge or clearing rough scrub-land. He would neither expect nor accept payment above and beyond a simple meal, usually at the Duck and Puddle; and he would simply melt away at the end of the day.

I have never mastered any of the poacher's skills, nor have I had any desire to do so, but I understand that to be a successful, professional poacher (that is to say one who succeeds in taking game enough for his own needs, with a few extra to sell, without being caught himself) you need a fine turn of speed, an ability to disappear into the undergrowth at the first sign of danger, even when there doesn't appear to be any, an understanding and a knowledge of your prey's habits and weaknesses and a unique ability to maintain a working relationship of some sort with local landowners, game-keepers and fish wardens.

If there was something which needed attention, but which required machinery or equipment, Toby would leave a message at the Duck and Puddle for the landowner concerned. If he found a blocked ditch or a dangerous dead tree, he would leave a message describing the site of the problem. He knew who owned every field, every hedge, every gate, every ditch and every stream in and around Bilbury.

It was hardly surprising that everyone in the area turned a blind eye to his activities. Mind you, it wouldn't have mattered if they hadn't condoned his presence: Toby had lived all his life in the country and knew every copse, every brook and every path. Even if someone had wanted to catch him they would have found it an impossible task.

Thumper once asked me how it could be considered stealing to take wild, living creatures from a field or a stream and I have to confess that I could see what he meant.

Much to the puzzlement of some of the locals (and for a long while to Patsy's parents), Patsy and I don't eat meat and I don't like the idea of animals being hunted and killed but, putting that aside, the fact is that rabbits and deer don't respect boundaries and it is difficult to see how they can possibly belong to a landowner in the same way that a tree or a blackberry bush can belong to someone.

As I have already said, I had never seen Toby professionally. He had never been to my consulting room in Bilbury Grange and I had never visited him. I didn't even know where he lived. I assumed, I think, that he lived in a hideaway somewhere in the woods; sheltering under some sort of rough concoction of old sacking and branches. If I had thought about it, I would have realised that it was a silly notion.

And then one day, Thumper came to see me at Bilbury Grange.

It was about 3.00 p.m. on a Sunday afternoon and the weather was foul. The sky was so dark with rain clouds that it could have been night. You could hear thunder occasionally and our animals, Ben the dog and our cats, were all crowded into a comfortable corner behind the sofa. Outside the house, the sheep were all gathered in the barn where they had been sheltering against the storm which they had known for a while was on its way. Sheep can smell bad weather coming long before you or I would know anything was amiss.

'Will you come and see Toby,' asked Thumper. He sounded upset and worried. 'I was in the woods an hour or so ago, passing his place and I thought I'd call in to see how he was. I hadn't seen him for a while.'

'What's happened to him?'

'He's been shot.'

I stared at Thumper disbelievingly. Who on earth would shoot Toby? 'Who shot him? What with? When? Why?'

'He was hit with a shotgun load. Last Saturday. Not yesterday, the Saturday before that. He doesn't know who shot him but he says he knows it wasn't deliberate. He says a fat man with a 12 gauge was blasting at everything in sight and that as he tried to get away from the area he was hit by a load from the gun. He says he thinks the man either fired low, because he'd seen a low flying bird, or that

42

he tripped and the gun went off accidentally. His back is peppered with shot and there is at least one buckshot pellet in his neck and another hit the back of his head. A couple of the damned things have come out. They're lead buckshot. I'd say they're size O or maybe even OO. Who the hell is using buckshot around here?'

I knew enough about shotgun cartridges to know that lead shot comes in a number of different sizes. Most hunters who are shooting rats or birds use small sized shot, and buckshot is usually kept for shooting big game animals such as deer. Buckshot which is size O is huge. Each lead ball is a third of an inch in diameter. Buckshot sized OO is even larger. The pellets are so large that a standard O gauge cartridge will contain only nine pellets.

And I realised immediately who had shot him.

Mr Chatterton, the idiot guest at the Pinchbecks' party who had been shot by his own gun, fired by a Labrador puppy, had been using a 12 gauge shotgun and he'd been using buckshot. He was as fat as they come; he had boasted to me that he weighed several hundredweight.

'How is he?'

'He's in a bad way, doc. If I hadn't happened to call in he would have just died there. He wouldn't go to the hospital and he wouldn't even come and see you. He certainly won't tell the police that he was shot.'

I picked up my bag. 'Did you tell him that you were going to fetch me?'

Thumper nodded.

'Was he OK about it?'

'He said he'd see you. But no ambulance. And he won't go into hospital. Not even the hospital in Bilbury. He said that if he's going to die then he wants to die at home.'

'Why won't he go into hospital?'

'He went into one once, a few years back. He said he heard them laughing at him. The nurses and the doctors treated him with contempt. He can't cope with being treated without respect.' Thumper paused and thought for a while. 'He's a man who has very little in his life. His dignity and his knowledge are important to him.'

It was, I think, one of the deepest and most sensitive things I'd ever heard Thumper say. He is usually a man of action rather than contemplation. I felt great sadness when Thumper told me this. I understood what he meant. And I felt sad that I knew that Toby's fear was probably justified.

'And he picked up a bad infection too,' said Thumper.

'He picked up an infection in the hospital?'

'Yes. Several actually. He nearly died from some bug he acquired while he was there. He had a bad time.'

'OK,' I said. 'So hospital isn't an option.'

Thumper insisted that we went in his truck. 'I can't get all the way to the cabin where he lives,' he explained. 'But I can get you much closer than you'll be able to get in your darned great Rolls Royce. It will still mean a half mile hike through the woods. So you'd better put on some boots and something warm and waterproof.'

I told Patsy where I was going and Thumper and I set off in his truck; a massive, beast of a four wheel drive vehicle which looks ungainly on ordinary roads but which can be driven over rougher ground than just about any other vehicle in North Devon. Thumper has put extra-large wheels onto the truck and this helps to increase the ground clearance. The exhaust pipe is connected to a pipe which blows waste gases out a foot above the roof of the cab. The truck can be driven through mud and water and can, I suspect, go places that would prove impassable even for a tractor.

It took us no more than fifteen minutes to reach the furthest spot in the wood that the truck could reach. From then on, we had to travel on foot. There was no easy path. Toby, a man who valued his privacy, had made sure that there was no clear track to his cabin. Every time he moved in or out, he took a slightly different route. There were roots and brambles everywhere. It occurred to me that if Toby needed to go to hospital, and could be persuaded to go there, we would have a hell of a job getting him out through the wood.

As we walked to Toby's cabin, Thumper explained that his friend had built the cabin himself, using a huge shipping crate as the basis for a structure which now blended into the forest so well that a wanderer could pass by just yards away without even knowing it was there. Toby had, said Thumper, taken the crate apart and then rebuilt it in a small clearing which he had made with nothing more than a handful of small tools and an old but sharp axe (a tool which Toby could use with such skill that he was able to make fence posts far quicker than men equipped with far more suitable equipment) and a

44

folding knife (a tool with which he could layer a hedge at a rate which even Thumper regarded as superhuman).

I discovered, rather to my surprise, that the crate was erected on land which belonged to Mr Kennet, Patsy's father, and that my father-in-law had happily given Toby permission to live on his land. In return, Toby repaired fences and gates throughout the Kennet acres. A month later, when I mentioned Toby to him, Mr Kennet admitted that he hadn't seen the poacher for eighteen months but that during that time he had never had to mend a fence or a gate or have a hedge re-layered.

Thumper had been right about Toby's tiny home. I don't know what I had expected to see; probably something along the lines of the cabin which Henry David Thoreau had built overlooking Walden Pond, on land owned by his friend Ralph Waldo Emerson. The very word 'cabin' carries notions of its own.

But this was nothing like Thoreau's cabin. It was so well hidden, so disguised, that I didn't see it at all until we were just yards away.

Toby had rebuilt the shipping crate and then grown ivy and other creepers around it and over it so well that it was as well hidden as any bird watchers' hide. There was no electricity and no water and no sewage, of course, but Toby didn't want the first, used a small, clear stream for the second and had a small shovel and several acres of woodland for the third.

Toby was lying on his face on a camp bed in his home, which was surprisingly roomy and tidy. There was a desk, a chair, an easy chair and a wash bowl and jug – the sort which used to be provided by small hotels and boarding houses before hotel rooms came with their own bathroom facility. The famous waxed coat was hanging on a hook which had been fastened to the back of the door. The place was dark, with the only light coming from the open doorway, until Thumper lit a couple of hurricane lamps which hung from hooks fixed into the walls. Pictures cut from magazines had been carefully pinned up. They were all of woodland scenes. The room stank of infection.

When Thumper announced our presence, Toby lifted himself onto one elbow and spoke, so quietly that I could hardly hear a word.

I leant closer.

He repeated what he'd said.

'Thumper shouldn't have brought you, doc,' he said. 'There's nothing you can do.' He sounded tired and resigned but not unhappy.

'Can I look?' I asked him.

'If you wish. Mind the ferret.'

I looked at Thumper.

'His ferret lives in his trouser pocket at the moment,' said Thumper. 'It won't bite if you don't disturb it.'

I carefully peeled the shirt from Toby's back. It must have been an incredibly painful process for him. His back was peppered with half a dozen holes. The pellets, I could see, were all still in his body. There was another one in his neck and a hole in the skin at the back of his skull showed where another of the shotgun pellets had smashed into his head. There was a piece of cord wrapped around Toby's neck. A brass key was hanging from the cord.

'The key to his Bible,' explained Thumper, without my having to ask. He sounded faint. Toby's back was certainly not a pretty sight. Every hole in Toby's back and neck was surrounded with dried blood and pus and the wounds stank of infection. I felt instantly that there could be no hope for him unless I could get him into hospital. And I knew that even then the chances of his recovering were slim. His body was feverish and he was intensely dehydrated. I suddenly realised that I didn't have the faintest idea how old he was. Like many folk who live rough in the country, it was difficult to tell. He could have been anywhere between 40 and 80.

When I looked at this brave lion of a man, my eyes were filled with tears of compassion and tears of hatred for the arrogant, ignorant, careless idiot who had done this to him – and who didn't even know what he had done.

'What can I do to help?' whispered Thumper. It was brave of him to offer. He had gone white.

For a while I didn't answer. I felt overwhelmed by a sense of sadness but there was much anger too. And most of all I didn't want to see him die.

I didn't know what I could do, let alone what Thumper could do to help me. I couldn't possibly clear out all those wounds without being able to give Toby a general anaesthetic. And how could I do that? And he needed antibiotics, that was clear.

'He has to go to hospital,' I whispered back.

'No hospital,' said Toby, who had heard my whisper. 'They'll call the police.'

'But you haven't done anything wrong,' I told him. 'The police won't do anything bad to you.'

'No police,' said Toby. I felt, rather than saw, Thumper leave the cabin.

'But I have to get you to hospital,' I repeated. I didn't mean to but in my desperation I put all the stress on the third word. 'If you stay here…' I didn't finish the sentence. It sounded too much like a threat.

'I'll die,' said Toby, finishing the sentence for me. He sounded frighteningly matter-of-fact about it. There was a fatalism about him which I found calming and disturbing at the same time.

'Yes, I'm afraid you will.' I said. The doctor in me felt that he had to know just how serious his condition was. The man in me knew that he was well aware that he was dying. He had spent all his life in a private world where death is a daily occurrence.

I could hear Thumper retching outside in the woods.

'Will you come to the hospital in Bilbury?' I asked him. 'Our little cottage hospital. I promise we won't call the police.'

'No hospitals,' said Toby again.

At that point, I really did not know what to do. I stood and looked and thought for what seemed an age. I heard Thumper come back into the cabin because the boards which made up the floor creaked underneath him.

'Sorry about that,' Thumper said softly.

I damned well didn't know what to do.

I felt full of sadness and frustration and rage and I felt utterly impotent and useless.

The trouble was that I understood why Toby wouldn't go into a hospital; I understood why he didn't trust hospitals, any hospital. I sometimes think that too many people are ready to go into hospital when they really don't have to. And there are, without a doubt, too many operations which aren't essential. But that may be because I know only too well how many things can go wrong. Back in the Middle Ages, people were genuinely afraid of hospitals. They knew that if they went into a hospital there was a very good chance that they would never come out again. Hospitals were places where people went to die. Even in the 19th century, things weren't much better; surgeons operated in frock coats and sharpened their scalpels on the soles of their boots.

Maybe it would be better if more people still felt more scepticism about hospitals.

There are a thousand reasons why hospitals can kill; patients die on the operating table, they contract serious infections and so on and on. Like many doctors, I am always astonished at how many people willingly submit themselves to the surgeon's knife for treatment which is optional or cosmetic.

And I think I understood why Toby was frightened of the police. His grandfather, a professional poacher and the man who had been Toby's mentor, had doubtless taught him that the police were his enemy.

But I knew that if Toby's wounds weren't cleaned then he would die. I knew that the huge lead buckshot pellets in his back had to be removed. His wounds needed to be dressed. He needed to be anaesthetised. He needed to have fluids and antibiotics administered through a drip. He needed to be in a sterile hospital, with fresh clean sheets on the bed. Damnit, he needed caring nurses looking after him 24 hours a day. He needed things I couldn't do for him. He needed help I couldn't give him. I could feel tears in my eyes. I admired Toby. I respected him. I liked him. I didn't know how old he was but it seemed clear to me that he had so much life left to live. He was a good, kind man who had probably never hurt any human being in his life. I couldn't help thinking of the fat oaf Chatterton; the careless, selfish, stupid, obscenely greedy man who had shot him.

And I wanted to call the police myself.

But I couldn't do that. Toby wouldn't want me to do that.

And even if I did tell the police, what would they do? Even if they managed to tie the incident to his gun, Chatterton would claim the shooting was an accident. He would probably say he tripped over a root. He would doubtless produce a licence and character references from half a dozen eminent members of the community. And Toby? They would dismiss him as an unlucky poacher. If it went to court, the defence counsel would probably argue that Toby deserved what he got. He shouldn't have been in the woods. What was he doing there? Poaching? Stealing pheasant? The end result would probably be that Chatterton would go scot-free and the police would arrest Toby.

Now it was my turn to go outside the cabin; out into the woods. I had never done anything like it before. Never walked out on a patient; albeit temporarily.

But I didn't go outside for the same reason as Thumper. I didn't feel nauseous. Already in my life I had seen too much, smelt too much, known too much, to be nauseated by the sight and smell of Toby's wounds.

But I felt I was about to burst with anger.

It was now dark. And it was pouring with rain. The forest seemed desperately unfriendly. I walked away a few yards, tripping over brambles and fallen branches. I kicked at one tree and then I punched another so hard that I hurt my hand. That knocked some sense into me. I walked back to the cabin.

I bent down and opened my black medical bag. I took out a pair of sterile rubber gloves and examined Toby's back as thoroughly as I could. He flinched when I touched him. I wasn't surprised. I'd have done more than flinch if my back had been that way and someone had touched it. Anyone would have flinched.

There were seven bullets still in his back. I could see all of them. There was one embedded in his neck. The one that had hit the back of his skull had bounced out. Shotgun blasts tend to produce most of their damage when the target is fairly close. Toby had clearly been standing almost at the extent of the gun's range. Dressed as he always was he would have been damned near invisible. That was no excuse for Chatterton firing a gun into the woods. But it was an explanation.

I took a scalpel and a pair of tweezers out of my bag and tried to remove one of the pieces of shot. It was tantalisingly close but I couldn't remove it. And the skin around the wounds was so damaged that there was nowhere for me to inject a local anaesthetic. I stood up. There seemed no alternative. If Toby was going to be saved then he would have to go into hospital.

Perhaps I could sedate him and then, with Thumper's help, carry him out of the cabin and out of the woods and take him, unknowing, to our cottage hospital. I could keep him sedated while I treated his back. And then we could take him back to his cabin when all the buckshot had been removed.

But that wasn't going to work.

For a start, it was technically a kidnapping.

And I couldn't just take Toby out of the woods against his will. He had already made it perfectly clear that he would rather die than go into hospital.

Could I certify him and have him taken to hospital regardless of his wishes?

That might work.

The authorities would certainly agree with me that a man who preferred to die than to be treated was not in his right mind.

But once again, I had to face the fact that Toby didn't want to go to hospital. He knew why. He knew what he was doing.

I took some dressings from my bag and bandaged his damaged back as best I could. And then I injected him with a large dose of a powerful antibiotic. I also gave him a modest dose of a decent painkiller.

As I did this I considered Toby's situation.

The main problem was clearly the need for an anaesthetic. If I could anaesthetise Toby then I could remove the buckshot from his back and neck. And I could clean out the wounds and dress the wounds properly. I could then put up a drip and give him regular blasts of antibiotic.

But how the devil could I anaesthetise him?

I couldn't anaesthetise him and manage the surgery he needed as well. I didn't even know much about anaesthesia. I'd never had any training in anaesthesia and never worked as an anaesthetist. I didn't have any equipment. I could inject him with a big dose of a tranquilliser. But that would be dangerous.

Or would it?

Maybe I could just inject him with something powerful enough to put him to sleep for a while, and then work on his back while he slept.

But I didn't like that idea very much. In fact, the more I thought about it the less I liked it.

It would be difficult to give him a big enough injection of a sedative without getting to the edge of a safe dose. And if I killed him with the anaesthetic I wouldn't be doing him much good. I wouldn't be doing myself much good, either. I'd probably find myself in front of a disciplinary tribunal at the General Medical Council. I'd be lucky not to be charged with manslaughter.

I needed outside help.

That was the big problem. I needed real help. I needed someone to manage the anaesthetic while I treated the wounds in Toby's back. And I needed someone to look after the drip and the antibiotics.

'Is there anything I can do?'

It was Thumper.

I turned to him. 'There might be.'

'Anything,' he said. 'I'll do anything you need me to do.'

'I need to go back to Bilbury Grange,' I told him. I'd had an idea. 'I need to make a phone call.'

'OK,' said Thumper.

'But I don't want to leave Toby here by himself.'

'I'll stay with him,' said Thumper immediately.

'I've given him a painkiller. He'll probably sleep for a while.'

'Good. That's good. Is there something you can do for him?'

'I'm working on it,' I told him. 'Fetch some water from the stream and if he wakes, try to get him to drink. He's terribly dehydrated.'

'OK.'

'Can I borrow your truck keys?'

Thumper took out the keys to his truck and handed them to me. 'Can you find your way to it?'

'Only if you tell me which direction to take when I leave the cabin. Otherwise there's a risk I'll be going round and round in circles for the rest of my life.'

Thumper came out and pointed out where the truck was parked. I could just see a corner of it through the trees.

'It'll be easier to back it out,' he told me. 'There's no room to turn it round.'

A short while later I was back at Bilbury Grange ringing my friend Will.

Will works as a GP in the English Midlands. I've known him for years and I would trust him with my life. We were at medical school together. He and his family come down to Bilbury from time to time. Before becoming a GP, Will took a postgraduate course in anaesthetics and for a while he considered becoming a professional anaesthetist. He still worked as an anaesthetist for a local emergency

51

service which helped the police deal with road accident casualty victims.

'I need a favour,' I told him. 'A big favour.'

'You've got it,' said Will without hesitation.

I explained the problem. I told him how I thought Toby had been injured. I explained who he was. I explained why he wouldn't go into hospital.

'I can remove the buckshot,' I told him. 'But I need a good gas man.'

'And you don't know one so you're asking me?'

'Something like that.'

'When do you need me?'

'As soon as you can get here.'

'I've nearly finished my evening surgery. I'll be done in twenty minutes. I can be there in three or four hours. Do you want to do it tonight?'

'The sooner the better.'

'Can we do it in the dark?'

'It'll be a bit tricky getting through the woods but there are a couple of hurricane lamps in the cabin.'

'Is it raining there?'

'Yes.'

'Good. I wouldn't want to feel let down. It always rains in North Devon.'

'Bring your waterproofs.'

'Will do. I'll also bring some hefty torches and a couple of heavy duty outside floodlights. We use them for roadside accidents. The batteries are pretty heavy though.'

'I can find someone to help carry the stuff,' I told him.

'I'll be with you as soon as I can. Do you want me to come to Bilbury Grange or do you need me to find this cabin in the woods?'

'Come to Bilbury Grange. You'll never find Toby's cabin.'

Will told me he'd be with me as soon as I could.

It did not escape my attention that he had never even asked who would pay for his expenses.

I broke the connection and dialled Patchy's number.

When he answered the phone I told him I needed help.

'When and where?' was all Patchy asked.

How fortunate I was to have such friends. Toby was pretty lucky too.

I told him.

'OK. What do you need?'

'I need your body and do you have one of those field radio things the army is always flogging off?'

'A two-way radio?'

'That's it.'

'No, I don't have one. But I know someone who has.'

'Can you borrow it?'

'Of course I can.'

I arranged for Patchy to come to Bilbury Grange in three hours' time – equipped with the borrowed two-way radio.

I then rang Flora and Camelia, a couple of the youngest of the helpers who assist in looking after patients at the Bilbury cottage hospital. Neither of them were professional nurses but they give their time freely and they are never flustered. We have a fine team of nurses helping out at the hospital. We have one regular nurse who is 82-years-old. If you met her you'd swear she couldn't be a day over 60. Most of our volunteer nurses give just one morning or afternoon a week but that's all we need from them. I asked the two I rang to ring others on our list to see if anyone else would help. I told them that I'd need them to work in two hour shifts. I told them I wanted them to stay in the cabin in pairs and explained that they would have a two-way radio so that they could stay in touch with me.

Flora and Camelia both promised to do everything they could to help. Everyone in the village knew Toby and although he was a loner, and perhaps not the easiest person to know, let alone to like, they all respected him and his chosen way of life.

If Toby wouldn't go into hospital then I would have to take the hospital to him.

I would have liked to ask Bradshaw, my ancient but indomitable practice nurse, and the matron of the Bilbury cottage hospital, but I didn't dare take him away from his regular work. He runs the hospital pretty well single-handedly. We had a couple of patients in the hospital at the time – one suffering from a nasty chest infection and the other recovering from a major operation performed at the big hospital in Exeter. I couldn't jeopardise their safety.

I asked the helpers I'd rung to come to Bilbury Grange.

If I was going to treat Toby in his cabin then someone had to be there 24 hours a day until he started to recover. And since I had surgeries to do, and the rest of the village to look after, that someone could not be me. I was going to need a rota of helpers. I just hoped that my part-time nurses would not find Toby's cabin in the woods too scary a place. The two-way radio would at least mean that no one staying there would feel completely isolated.

Finally, after explaining to Patsy what I'd arranged, I drove round to the cottage hospital, still in Thumper's truck and picked up all the equipment I thought I would need: a drip stand, saline drip bottles and more antibiotics. I also picked up a variety of swabs and some more sophisticated equipment than the sort of things I usually carried in my medical bag.

When I'd done all this, I drove Thumper's truck back to the woods where Toby's cabin was situated. I carried all the stuff I'd collected with me through the woods. It was now pitch dark and still raining heavily. I had also taken with me a scythe I'd picked up from Bilbury Grange. I used it to help clear a rough path through the brambles.

'Sorry I left you so long,' I said to Thumper. 'How is he?'

I piled the stuff I'd brought with me into a corner of the cabin.

'He's been sleeping most of the time. He's sort of woken up a couple of times. He doesn't seem any better I'm afraid. He's been confused and a bit delirious.'

I took Thumper outside into the rain and explained what I was planning and who I had recruited to help me.

'You and Will are going to operate on him here?'

'Can you think of an alternative?'

'No, but...'

'If I don't do this then he will die. So we don't have anything to lose, do we?'

'No, I guess not.' Thumper paused and looked at me. 'But are you allowed to do this? Is it legal?'

I shrugged. I didn't have the faintest idea whether or not my planning to operate on Toby in his cabin was legal or not. I suspected that 'not' was probably the answer. But I couldn't see an alternative and laws are often made by people who cannot possibly know whether or not they are always going to be 'right'.

I asked Thumper if he could wait at the cabin for a little longer because I had to go back to Bilbury Grange to wait for Patchy, my part-time nurses and for Will. We couldn't do anything until Will arrived.

'Give me the scythe,' said Thumper. 'While you're gone I'll clear a proper path to the cabin. When Toby finds out what I've done he will hate the idea of having a path through the woods but he'll just have to put up with it!'

I thanked him, hurried back to his four wheeled drive truck and then drove again to Bilbury Grange. I liked Thumper's confidence. Privately, I thought my chances of saving Toby's life were considerably less than fifty-fifty.

On my way back, the rain slowed a little and I think it even stopped for a couple of minutes. But the clouds soon thought better of it and within another five minutes the damned stuff was coming down as though God had realised he'd made too much rain and had decided to deplete his stocks a little. There was so much cloud that there was no moon visible. The night was pitch black – just perfect for carrying equipment out to a cabin in the woods when there was no discernible path to follow.

Still, I thought, if it were easy where would be the challenge?

I couldn't help smiling as that thought occurred to me.

That was a favourite saying of Dr Brownlow, my predecessor, my friend and my mentor. Always delivered tongue in cheek with a twinkle in his eyes.

Will arrived just before 9.30 p.m. that evening. We quickly fed and watered him, for the poor soul had come straight from his evening surgery, and then he, I, Patchy and two of the Bilbury cottage hospital's finest young amateur nurses (Camelia, the younger one was 44 and Flora, the older one, was in her 70s) piled into Thumper's truck. Will had brought two boxes full of equipment, which turned to be even heavier than it looked, and Patchy had the field radios which had probably been state of the art cutting technology in 1941 but which we tested and which still worked perfectly well.

Thumper had carved an approximation of a path through the wood. He was soaked, scratched and starving hungry. I handed him the packet of sandwiches and the thermos flask which Patsy had made up for him.

'I told her she was treating you like a big softie,' I told him as I handed over the packet and the flask. He thanked me and said that when he'd finished helping us carry the equipment to the cabin he would sit in his truck for a while and eat his supper. Thumper is surprisingly queasy when it comes to blood. Patchy, who is also not wild about the goriest aspects of medical care, said he would keep him company.

By the time we had set up Will's lights, and spread out our equipment, the inside of Toby's cabin looked like a field hospital.

Poor Toby, who was still woozy from the injections I had given him, awoke and looked around. I explained that he was going to be anaesthetised and that I was going to remove the buckshot from his body. He didn't really seem to know what was going on or why.

Will erected a drip stand, put up a drip and started pumping saline into Toby's veins. Anaesthetists can slip a needle into a vein far more skilfully than anyone else. When I was at medical school, I remember that a crowd of us spent over an hour one Saturday afternoon trying to put a needle into an infant who needed a drip. Three students, a house physician, a house surgeon, a junior registrar, two senior registrars and a consultant paediatrician had all tried and failed. There didn't seem to be a vein left that hadn't been temporarily ruined by all the bodging and piercing. In the end, we telephoned for a paediatric anaesthetist to come and see if he could succeed where we had all failed. He came in wearing appalling golfing garb. He had been standing on the first tee when he'd been given our message. He walked up to the patient and within fewer seconds than it takes to write this sentence, he had slipped a needle into a vein. 'Is that all?' he asked, looking round. When no one spoke, he marched back out again. His playing partners were probably still playing their approach shots to the green when he returned to his game.

Just as I was about to start washing Toby, and everything else in sight, with vast quantities of a heavy duty antiseptic solution, Thumper pushed open the door.

'Have you moved the ferret out of Toby's pocket?'

We hadn't, of course.

'How could you forget?' asked Will with mock indignation. 'I seem to remember that de-ferreting the patient was the first thing they taught us at medical school.'

After explaining to Toby that he would look after his ferret, Thumper removed the animal from the trouser pocket which, judging by the way it clung to the lining, it had adopted as its temporary home. Judging by the yells and curses which were involved, I thought it fair to assume that Thumper had received a couple of nips. The two nursing aides who were in the cabin with us backed up to the edge of the cabin as the ferret was being extracted. I would have done the same if I hadn't been worried that everyone would think me a townie wuss if I did.

'I'll keep him safe for you,' Thumper promised Toby. I'm not sure that Toby heard or understood him. 'I've got a box in the back of the truck,' he told me. 'I'll look after the ferret until Toby is better.'

I liked Thumper's quiet confidence that Toby would get better. I was still nervous and full of doubts. The infection which we had to treat had taken a real hold and we would only succeed if the antibiotic I'd selected proved to be effective.

When Will and I had gone outside to discuss our plan of attack, he had agreed that he wouldn't put Toby's chances at much better than 50:50.

'What antibiotic have you started him on?' asked Will.

I told him.

'Good choice. That's the one I'd have picked. Excellent broad spectrum drug. What dose?'

I told him.

'Let's pile some more into the drip bottle. He's going to need buckets of the stuff if we're going to kill this infection. If anything kills him it will be the bugs not the bullets.'

I have to say that it was a pleasure to work with Will. He was a marvel. Calm, never fussy, never panicky; he skilfully anaesthetised Toby and kept him under while I worked.

The battery run emergency lights which he had brought with him were marvellous too. As far as the lighting was concerned, it was like working in a proper operating theatre.

Camelia and Flora, the two nursing aides, gloved and masked, were also wonderful. They may not have received any formal nursing training (I didn't tell Will until later but Camelia was a former hairdresser and Flora had been a teller in a bank) but they did everything I needed them to do and they did it with surprising efficiency and with good grace.

It took me half an hour to remove all the buckshot (Will was right to call the damned things bullets for they were so big they looked more like bullets than shot) and ping them into the metal kidney dish which Flora, one of the aides, held out for me.

Actually, no, I am going to call them 'nurses'. They may not have been trained 'nurses' but they did the work of nurses and they did it calmly and professionally.

And then it took another twenty minutes to sew up the holes the bullets had made. I then poured on more antiseptic solution before taping some dressings over the wounds. The cabin now reeked of antiseptic. It was preferable to the smell of infection.

By the time I'd finished, I was soaked with sweat and beginning to shake from the tension of concentrating so hard. Not even country GPs do a lot of extensive surgery. We sew up cuts and so on but the stuff that needs a proper surgeon usually needs a proper hospital.

'You can bring him round when you're ready,' I told Will wearily.

'I thought you were going to be here all night!' he said. 'Have you finished at last? What have you been doing? Liver transplant was it?'

It is a common and traditional conceit of anaesthetists everywhere to appear to have absolutely no interest in what the operating surgeon is doing.

'Simple sex change op,' I told him. 'All finished now.'

The two nurses, who were busy tidying up the instruments and counting the swabs I had used (to make sure that I hadn't left any inside Toby when I had sewn him up) looked up and seemed shocked. I realised that neither of them had ever worked in a proper operating theatre.

'Sorry,' I apologised. 'It's been a bit tense.'

'Is he going to be all right?' asked Flora.

I looked at her, wondering what the hell to tell her.

And then I realised that she and her colleagues would be looking after Toby for the next few days. I needed them to believe that Toby would get better. I wanted them to be optimistic and upbeat.

'He's going to be fine,' I told her with false confidence. Camelia, who was shaking noticeably, smiled with relief.

58

Will looked at me and then, understanding, nodded almost imperceptibly.

It was so good to have him there.

Will and I agreed that it would be best to keep Toby sedated for 48 hours or so while his body recovered a little. Toby was tough but his body needed plenty of rest in order to recover properly. I was also worried that if he woke up and found strangers in his cabin he might try to get out of bed and disrupt the drip tube which was feeding him essential fluid and medication. I catheterised him so that his bladder could be kept drained.

We fixed up a rota system so that there would always be someone in the cabin with Toby. Thumper, Patchy and I divided up the night time into three sessions and the nurses we had recruited stayed with him in pairs during the day time. I needed the nurses to be in pairs because Toby was a strong fellow and if he awoke, confused and frightened, I didn't want one of them to be there alone.

Will and I showed the others how to change the drip bags so that Toby was kept hydrated and we showed them how to inject the antibiotics and sedatives directly into each new bag of fluid. We set up the two-way radio so that whoever was in the cabin would always be able to contact the outside world. Apart from changing the fluid bottles, adding drugs to the fluid bottles and occasionally emptying the bottle into which the catheter was draining, there wasn't much for anyone to do.

It was just a question of waiting.

Waiting to see if Toby's body would recover from the massive insults it had received.

And waiting to see if the antibiotic I had prescribed would do its job and kill the bacteria which had invaded his body.

Will stayed at Bilbury Grange for the rest of what was left of the night. After no more than a couple of hours rest, he got up at 5 a.m. to drive back to the Midlands in order to conduct his morning surgery. He refused point blank to allow me to pay for the petrol his car had consumed. I promised to ring him later in the day to let him know how Toby was doing. Patsy packed him up some sandwiches and a flask of hot coffee and told him he had to stop at least once en route for a short break.

I went back to the cabin at the end of my morning surgery and again in the middle of the afternoon. Without Thumper's truck to take me deep into the woods, I had to leave the Rolls Royce parked some distance away and walk further along the rough track that led into the woods. Thanks to Thumper's work with a scythe, there was now a decent path to the cabin. I couldn't help thinking that Toby wasn't going to be at all happy when he discovered that there was now a walkway through the woods. Still, if he was unhappy about the pathway, he would at least be alive. And the woodland brambles and other undergrowth would soon grow back. On my trip that afternoon I realised that I was beginning to know my way into the woods.

Toby was still sleeping.

And I was delighted when I realised, when I changed the dressings on his back, that I could not smell any infection. Indeed, I was excited to see that the wounds looked a little better. The redness around the entry holes made by the buckshot was beginning to fade. We weren't 'out of the woods' as people say in such circumstances, but I really believed that Toby now stood a real chance of making a full recovery. I rang Will and told him that I thought Toby's chances were now 75% rather than the much less optimistic 50% we had previously estimated. He sounded tired but elated. He had a right to be tired. In addition to acting as unpaid anaesthetist for Toby's operation, he had spent nearly eight hours driving. It was quite a relief to know that he had got home safely and without a speeding ticket.

The following day, I was so pleased with how things were going that I removed the catheter and stopped the sedative. I removed the drip and made sure that Thumper and I were the only two people in the cabin when Toby awoke. Toby would still need the antibiotics, of course, but he could take these by mouth instead of via a drip bottle.

'Where's my ferret?' asked Toby, when he woke. Those were his first words.

'He's at my place,' said Thumper. 'I'm looking after him for a few days.'

'Why?' demanded Toby.

I tried to explain that having a ferret in a hospital recovery room was not generally accepted to be a good idea. Naturally, Toby neither understood nor accepted this. Rather than see my patient become unduly agitated I told Thumper that he could take the ferret back to the cabin.

I had planned for Toby to stay in his cabin for another two or three days. I wanted his body to have a proper chance of recovering before he went out into the big, wide world.

I shouldn't have been surprised when Toby rejected this advice.

We were able to abandon the nursing rota far sooner than I had expected. I made Toby swear that he would take the antibiotics I had prescribed, and twice a day I changed his dressings.

It had been quite a medical adventure.

Two weeks later, Will brought his family down for a weekend. I took Will round to the woodland cabin to see how our patient was recovering.

Toby didn't know who Will was, of course, but when I explained that Will had driven a round trip of nearly 400 miles in order to help with his operation, there were tears in the poacher's eyes.

'You did that for me!' he said. 'But you don't know me...'

'No,' said Will. 'I don't know you.' He then pointed at me. 'But I know him.'

'I've never had a friend like that,' said Toby softly.

'Oh, I think you've got more friends than you thought you had,' said Will with a smile.

King Charles II's Bed

Patchy was celebrating the sale of King Charles II's bed and was treating us all to champagne. We had one opened bottle in an ice bucket and another bottle cooling in Frank's refrigerator. Frank always keeps a few bottles of decent champagne in his cellar, though I suspect we are the only people in the village who ever drink the stuff. And we only ever drink it when Patchy has made a good sale.

A Japanese buyer had paid the asking price for the bed and had handed over the cash up front in a smart pigskin briefcase. Patchy had come to the Duck and Puddle immediately after supervising the packing of the purchase into a crate, the loading onto a lorry and the start of its journey across the world.

He had, he said, made a 'satisfactory' profit.

'Why the dickens did someone in Japan want to buy a bed that Charles II had slept in?' asked Thumper.

'I don't have the foggiest notion,' replied Patchy with disarming honesty. 'It's as much a puzzle to me as it is to you.' He raised a glass. 'But I drink to the Japanese! Wonderful people and connoisseurs of objects d'art.'

We drank to the Japanese.

Even Frank, whose alcohol intake is strictly monitored by his wife, was allowed to drink champagne. Gilly had agreed that champagne, consisting largely of bubbles, cannot be considered a proper alcoholic beverage and should, rather, be classified as a sort of upmarket fizzy pop.

'Is it a particularly handsome bed?' I asked.

'No, not really,' admitted Patchy. 'To look at, it's a fairly ordinary four poster bed. But it's made out of solid oak and it weighs a ton. Fortunately, it comes apart so two or three hefty fellows can move it. I've sent instructions on how to put it all back together so, hopefully, they'll be able to turn the bits into a bed without too much difficulty when it finally gets to Japan.'

'Is it an especially comfortable bed?' asked Thumper. 'Goose feather mattress? That sort of thing?'

'The mattress had long since expired so I had to have one made up by a mattress craftsman,' explained Patchy. 'It's a very short bed, of course, because the people weren't very tall in the days of Charles II. The mattress had to be specially made.'

'It'll be fine for the Japanese, though, I guess,' said Frank.

We looked at him.

'Them being smallish sized people,' explained Frank. He held a hand about five feet off the floor to indicate what he meant. 'On the whole.'

'Yes, I suppose they are,' said Patchy. 'I hadn't thought of that. Actually, I hadn't really thought that anyone would ever sleep in it. To be honest they could have bought a really nice, brand new bed for a fraction of the price. Given the historical connections, it's more the sort of thing you have on display in a museum. I think the chap who bought it has a small private museum. He's in banking, absolutely loaded, and I've sold him one or two other things: a desk that Shakespeare wrote on, an axe that was used by Henry VIII's executioner, a pen that was used by King John, the monarch who signed the Magna Carta.' He waved his glass about airily. 'And a few more things of that ilk.'

Thumper and I nodded.

We all knew the truth.

Patchy knew we knew the truth.

And we knew that he knew that we knew the truth. But some things are best left unsaid.

Patchy is very careful these days. When he says that King Charles II has slept in a bed he doesn't say how many nights he spent in it. When he says that Shakespeare used a desk he doesn't say it was the only desk Shakespeare ever used. The axe wasn't necessarily the one that Henry VIII's executioner used when decapitating Queens of England. The pen that was used by King John wasn't necessarily the one with which he signed the Magna Carta.

This caution has solid business reasoning behind it. If you sell King Charles II's bed, implying that it was his only bed, then you can only sell it once. If you simply claim that the bed was one in which the King spent a night then your opportunities are almost endless. With 365 nights a year, and a King who was known to have wandered the country about a good deal, there must be hundreds of beds around which can rightfully claim to have provided comfort and support for the Royal personage.

To be honest I was in awe of Patchy's skill, and I suspect that Thumper and Frank were too. I do not for one moment believe that I would ever have the courage to do what he did and although it might, I suppose, be considered morally rather dubious by some people, I found it impossible to criticise him or think badly of him.

And this was not just because Patchy was my good and loyal friend, and my brother-in-law, but because I knew him to be a quiet benefactor who unostentatiously helped many in the village. Some philanthropists like to be very public about their good deeds; often promising far more than they ever give. But Patchy was the opposite; invariably giving far more than he ever promised. He has far more of the Robin Hood about him than he would ever lay claim to, or even admit to.

I knew that if I ever came across a patient who was in genuine need, but who had fallen between the support lines of the State, I could appeal to Patchy on their behalf. Right from the start, he had been a generous donor to the Bilbury Cottage Hospital.

'Don't you have any difficulty getting this sort of stuff out of the country?' asked Thumper, disingenuously. 'I thought the authorities were pretty firm about keeping national treasures in the country.'

'Ah, well, there's a way round all that,' said Patchy. 'I don't actually put down what the item is on the customs forms. With the bed, I just said it was a second-hand bed. With Shakespeare's desk, I always put it down as a 'desk'. And similarly the axe is just an axe and the pen is just a pen. I never have any problems.'

'That's quite handy,' said Thumper with a grin. 'If, heaven forbid, anyone were to claim that the bed hadn't been slept in by Charles II, you could just point to the customs form which says it's just an old, second-hand bed.'

'Gosh I suppose so,' said Patchy, as though this were a thought that had never crossed his mind. He sipped more of the celebratory champagne. 'I hadn't thought of that.'

We sat for a while and drank several toasts to the bed and to the Japanese banker who was paying for our champagne. Frank said that when a dear friend has had a piece of good fortune it is only gentlemanly to help him celebrate.

Frank had just tipped the final remains of the second bottle of champagne into Patchy's glass when we heard a commotion on the forecourt outside the Duck and Puddle. We looked out to see a coach discharging its cargo: a team of Morris dancers. They were all dressed in white trousers and white shirts and wore surprisingly hefty looking boots. They had red handkerchiefs around their necks and rings of bells strapped to their lower legs.

Moments later, a dozen or more hefty looking men, all in their middle years and all obviously on the well-fed side of hungry, jingled and jangled their way into the pub. Some of them collected around the bar. Most sat down here and there wherever there were spaces. One, I noticed, started shouting orders to Frank.

'We're on our way to South Molton,' one of the dancers told me. 'But we thought we'd stop off on the way for something refreshing.'

He was red faced, notably overweight and already sweating with the exertion of climbing down from the coach and walking into the pub. I had no idea how he was going to dance his way through an energetic Morris dancing set without collapsing. If he'd been an old shirt you would have torn him up to use as rags.

'Where have you come from?' I asked the red-faced dancer, expecting to hear that they had travelled from Cornwall or Somerset.

'Combe Martin,' came the reply.

'But that's only a couple of miles down the road!'

'Indeed, you are right,' said the red-faced dancer. 'And it is, to be almost exact, just under 19 miles from Combe Martin to South Molton. But we have been advised that, given our age and physical condition, we should take the risk of dehydration very seriously. So whenever we see a pub we always stop for a drink.'

'Quite wise,' I nodded. And then, after thinking about it for a moment, I added: 'But the Duck and Puddle isn't really on the road you'd normally take if you were set out to drive from Combe Martin to South Molton.'

'You are undoubtedly correct about that too. But Edgar, our driver, has no sense of direction,' said the red-faced dancer rather sadly. 'He's 93 and been known to get lost in his own house.'

I looked out of the window and could see the driver, who was still on the coach, pouring himself a cup of tea from a thermos flask. He had a bad tremor and seemed to be spilling more of the stuff than he managed to decant into the cup.

'He looks frail,' I said.

'He is, he is,' said the red-faced dancer. 'He's had a hard life. More bad breaks than that bloke Job in the Bible – you know, the one with the boils and so on. You name the disease and he's probably had it, got it or sickening for it. But he says he likes working for us because if he's working he knows he's not dead yet. He's not a member of our club but he's the only person we know who'll do the driving without the drinking. We buy him a pie and a bottle of pop at lunchtime and a bag of chips and a nice piece of haddock at the end of the day and he's as happy as Larry to get out and about a bit. The only thing is that his eyes are pretty terrible and he broke his glasses a couple of months ago so we take it in turns to sit up at the front and give him instructions. We tell him when to turn and warn him if there's any traffic around or a bend coming up. It works very so well.'

I looked at him, wondering if I was having my leg pulled. I must have looked a little startled.

'Don't look so worried! He's pretty well perfectly safe,' protested the red-faced dancer, who was clearly not joking. He gratefully accepted a pint of traditional ale which was handed to him by one of his colleagues. I watched in astonishment as the pint disappeared in a single gulp.

'My brother-in-law used to do the driving for us,' continued my new and temporary companion. 'He's an alcoholic so he tries not to drink too much booze – just beer and cheap wine. But he and I don't always see eye to eye so he now dances with some Morris Dancers over in Lynton. Anyway, as they say, relations are like cow's muck – best when well spread around.'

I sipped at my own drink.

Suddenly a group of his fellow dancers started to sing. It was, I quickly realised, the first verse of a popular choral work known as Eskimo Nell. I wondered if the Morris Dancers knew the other 75 unauthorised verses.

These were men whose days were doubtless full of rates demands, blocked plumbing, hedges which required trimming and 14-year-old daughters who needed to be transported to their ballet class.

But for the time being, they were clearly content to live for pleasure alone.

66

And who could blame them?

The proceedings of the day had begun and the day was now well and truly set in motion.

'Last month we set off to dance at some fete or show or something in Cornwall but we never got there,' continued my red-faced companion. 'Our intentions were good but we were so careful to make sure that we didn't get dehydrated that we didn't get any further than the Red Lion in Bideford. Someone worked out that we were 112 miles short of our destination when we turned back.'

The member of the troupe who had been handing out the beers now handed out home-made pasties. He was carrying a tray piled high with them. It occurred to me that Gilly must have known that the Morris dancers were due to stop in for light sustenance and dehydration prevention.

'Paul is our designated orderer,' explained the red-faced man, taking his pasty. 'We find it makes life easier if one of us does the ordering in pubs. We all eat and drink the same. We're not fussy eaters.'

It certainly seemed to be an efficient system.

'Aren't those boots a trifle heavy for dancing?' I asked him, looking down at what looked like ex-army boots. The leather had clearly been well treated with dubbin and both boots were equipped with heavy steel toecaps.

'You could well be right about that,' said the red-faced dancer, taking a large, hungry man's bite out of his pasty. 'Excuse me having a bit of a snack,' he said, spraying crumbs about, 'but I've not eaten since breakfast.'

'You go ahead,' I told him. 'The engine must be fuelled.'

The red-faced dancer nodded and took another large bite of his pasty. At this rate, a baked delicacy the size of a normal dinner plate would be gone in three bites. For normal people, one of Gilly's pasties requires a knife and a fork and twenty minutes of careful slicing and eating.

'The boots is a mite heavy for dancing,' admitted the red-faced dancer, going back to my previous question. 'But they're just right for kicking.'

'Kicking?' I asked, puzzled. I knew that in Gloucestershire the locals are particularly fond of a sport called 'shin kicking', a curious activity in which, as the name suggests, protagonists kick one

67

another's shins until one admits defeat and is trundled off to the first aid tent for sympathy and a warm poultice. But I had never before heard that shin kicking was a favoured part of the Morris Dancer's repertoire.

'Sometimes, on our travels around, we finds that we gets clever clogs who likes to take the mickey,' he said. 'Likes to have a bit of a laugh at our expense.'

'Not something you favour?'

He laughed. 'Definitely not something we favour. We have a tendency to discourage that sort of thing.'

'And the boots come in handy?'

'The boots definitely come in handy. They have their disadvantages in that they weigh a bit more than a nice dancing slipper, say, but they has their advantages in that when you get one of those colliding with your shin, your inclination to have a bit of a laugh at someone else's expense tends to dissipate.'

'Dissipate?'

'That's it. That's the word. Dissipate. We may look simple folk but deep down we is educated peoples you know.'

'I definitely don't doubt it,' I said. 'I wouldn't even doubt it if you weren't wearing those boots. But since you are wearing those boots I most definitely don't doubt it.'

'I can see you're a wise man, sir,' said the red-faced dancer.

The man who was handing out drinks and food brought my new friend another pint of beer and another pasty. These were accepted eagerly, as though they were the first sustenance to be seen for some days. I have to say I was impressed. When I have eaten one of Gilly's pasties I don't usually need, or want, to eat again for 24 hours. The Morris Dancers' choral group now moved on to another verse in the seemingly endless saga describing the activities of Eskimo Nell. I reckoned they were on about verse seven.

'We'll be off soon, and we'll leave you and your friends in peace,' said the red-faced dancer. He took a swig from his pint mug and a bite from his second pasty. 'We've four more refreshment stops to make before we get to South Molton.'

I stared at him in admiration.

'We have to keep in shape,' he said.

'Absolutely,' I agreed.

'Bertie jogs for us twice a week.'

Puzzled, I looked at him.

'Bertie,' he nodded towards a tall, unusual thin dancer near the bar.

'He jogs for you?'

'Sure. He's our nominated jogger. You know how people going out to a pub have a nominated driver? The poor sod who agrees not to drink so that he can drive back home.'

'I've heard of it,' I admitted. It was not, I'm afraid, something that had caught on in Bilbury.

'Well, Bertie is our nominated jogger. He jogs for us. It saves the rest of us having to do it.'

'That's a splendid idea,' I said, for I truly thought it was.

'It wouldn't be safe for a man like me to go jogging.'

'No, you're right, it wouldn't.'

'People fall dead while jogging.'

'They do. Indeed they do.'

'So by having a nominated jogger we avoid all that risk. It's safer all round. You could say it saves lives.'

'Absolutely. I understand.'

'Mind you, I do a little exercise myself occasionally,' said my new chum. 'I did a press up a few months ago. It was for a bet.'

'Just the one?'

'It's not one of those things you want to do more than once is it?'

'I guess not.'

My new chum suddenly noticed that there was still a chunk of pastry on his plate. 'Pity to waste that,' he said. He picked up the pastry and popped it into his mouth.

Suddenly, without saying anything, he leapt to his feet and rushed off, heading for the gents. This was clearly not the first time he and his companions had visited the Duck and Puddle.

I watched him go, assuming at first that he needed to get rid of some of his beer.

But something hadn't seemed quite right.

So, after a few seconds delay, I hurried after him.

I found him in the pub's back yard, on his knees, struggling for breath. He had gone a rather nifty shade of blue and he was clearly choking. I guessed that the last piece of pie had stuck in his windpipe.

I opened his mouth and looked inside; hoping that I might be able to reach the obstruction and pull it out. But I could see no blockage. I was about to reach for my penknife to perform an emergency tracheotomy, in an attempt to bypass the blockage, when I suddenly remembered that a year or two earlier I met a doctor at an anti-vivisection conference who told me about a technique he had devised for helping individuals who were choking. I couldn't remember the doctor's name but I remembered his enthusiasm for his new technique.

I decided that now was the time to try it out. I desperately tried to remember what the doctor had told me.

'Can you get to your knees?'

The Morris Dancer struggled up to his knees.

'Can you now stand up?'

Holding onto a conveniently placed drainpipe, he pulled himself up to his feet.

I then stood behind the Morris Dancer, who looked like death warmed up and was definitely no longer red faced, put my arms around him, grasped one fist with the other hand, put the two joined fists into the space just below his sternum and pulled sharply.

Nothing happened.

I tried it again.

And this time the piece of pie crust came flying out of the man's mouth, freeing his windpipe for its proper purpose.

He coughed, coughed again and then took a deep breath.

I remembered the name of the man who had taught me this technique: it was Dr Heimlich. I decided that I should send him a note to tell him that his technique had worked and saved the life of an English Morris Dancer.

'Crumbs,' croaked the dancer. 'That was a close call. Thank heavens you came outside and found me. If you hadn't happened along I'd have been dead.'

'Why did you go outside?' I asked him.

'I thought I was going to have to bring up that piece of pastry that had got stuck. I didn't want to do it in a room full of people.'

'But you should never leave the room if you're choking!' I told him.

We stayed outside for a few minutes while he recovered. A seagull swooped down and picked up the piece of pie crust. By the time we went back into the pub, the rest of the troupe of Morris Dancers were heading for the door. They were still singing lustily about the awesome exploits of the hardworking Eskimo Nell.

'Thank you, friend,' said the man who'd been choking.

'Pleasure,' I told him.

A minute later, their coach pulled away from the Duck and Puddle. There was much crunching of the gears as the 93-year-old driver found one which the engine considered suitable for starting off on the next leg of its journey. I noticed that a member of the dancing troupe was sitting beside Edgar, clearly giving him directions and guiding him from the Duck and Puddle forecourt.

'Crumbs!' said Frank, wiping his forehead with the tea-towel he used to wipe up the bar counter. 'The pub feels empty and quiet without that lot.'

'That's probably because it is empty and quiet,' Thumper pointed out.

'Hadn't thought of that,' said Frank. He started to collect the empty glasses. 'Still, we do good business when the Morris Dancers stop by. They're always thirsty and hungry. It must be all that dancing around waving their hankies.'

From the conversation I'd just had, I wasn't convinced that the Morris Dancers who had just called in at the Duck and Puddle ever got round to doing much dancing.

Now that it was quiet, we could hear that Patchy was on the telephone.

'I need another two of those Charles II's beds,' said Patchy to the person on the other end of the line. 'I've sold the next one to a Russian customer who has bought it sight – unseen and I've got three customers from Hong Kong fighting for the right to buy the next one.'

The person at the other end of the telephone said something I didn't hear.

'I need the first one by next Friday, and the other one by the end of the month,' said Patchy, putting down the receiver. He suddenly realised I was there and looked a trifle embarrassed. He called to Frank who was in the Duck and Puddle kitchens with Gilly. 'How much do I owe you for the call?'

'Local, national or international?'

'Birmingham.'

71

'That sounds like 'international' but it's on the house,' shouted Frank.

'Why not sell a bed to each of the customers in Hong Kong?' I asked Patchy.

'Oh no, no,' said Patchy. 'I have a simple rule. Never sell the same seemingly exclusive, almost entirely unique historical artefact to more than one person in a country.' He paused and then a slight smile crossed his lips. 'Not at the same time anyway.'

'What's the time?' asked Thumper.

Frank squinted at the clock – which is still not working. 'It's probably a quarter to something,' he said. 'I find it's often quarter to something. Or sometimes quarter past something.' He announced this as though it were useful information. In Bilbury, it is generally thought that the 'something' rarely matters as much as people think it ought to.

'Just time for another round then,' said Thumper.

'And maybe a cheese and onion roll,' suggested Patchy.

We all decided we'd each like a cheese and onion roll.

'They were nice blokes, those Morris Dancers,' said Thumper.

'But I prefer them when they're not here,' said Patchy.

'They're very noisy,' I said. 'What with those bells they wear tinkling every time they move and those boots they wear being a bit on the clunky side, they make more noise than a crowd of school kids.'

'And they're all so big they seem to fill the place,' said Patchy.

'Good for business, though,' said Frank. 'I take more when they come in than I normally take in a month of Sundays.'

We all looked at him.

'Sundays are our best day,' explained Frank. 'People go out for a drive or a walk on Sundays. And since someone took down all the road signs, they get lost. They come in to find out where they are and while they're in here they usually buy something. Even if they're not hungry or thirsty they feel they ought to buy something because I've been so nice and helpful.'

'Are you nice and helpful?' asked Thumper.

'Of course,' said Frank. 'I'm always nice and helpful.'

'Where are our drinks?' asked Patchy.

'Get 'em yourselves,' said Frank. 'You know where everything is. What do you think I am? A bloody slave or something.'

And so while Frank tottered off to make the cheese and onion rolls we all helped ourselves to drinks and Thumper, who said he'd pay for them, put an IOU into the till.

A Guest Called Spike

Thumper was at Bilbury Grange collecting manure which he intended to sell to a market garden the other side of Barnstaple. Farmyard manure is regarded by gardeners as the best fertiliser for plant growth. It contains minerals and trace elements and many bacteria and fungi which help plants grow. It also contains auxins from urine and nitrogen and phosphoric acid. People who know about these things tell me that no garden is complete without a steady supply of auxins, nitrogen and phosphoric acid.

Large farm animals produce fairly impressive quantities of manure.

A cow or a horse will produce around five tons of manure a year each and Cedric, the pig which we look after for our American friends who won the 'Bowling for the Pig' competition at the Duck and Puddle, produces about a ton of manure every year. That's a lot of manure, and although we use quite a bit of it ourselves, we cannot possibly use a ton of manure in every 12 month period.

Thumper gets rid of the excess manure for us, and the price he receives from the market garden covers his petrol costs and leaves him with a modest profit. Thumper earns his living via a huge variety of schemes which earn him a little profit here and a little profit there. If he worked in the city, he would say that he had a portfolio of jobs. Since he works in Bilbury, he just has a number of little jobs which earn him a bit here and a bit more there.

I was helping shovel some of Cedric's food waste into the back of Thumper's truck when he asked me if I'd heard the latest wonderful story about our mutual friend Peter Marshall, who runs the village shop in Bilbury.

Thumper told me that Samuel Houghton, a local farmer, has a regular order for a magazine called *Tractor Times*. This is, as the name rather suggests, a periodical devoted to the study of tractors. There may be the occasional feature about ploughs in the magazine but it is a magazine in which the tractor plays a starring role. I have seen several copies, and as a country doctor with a rural practice, I usually have one or two recent editions on the table in my waiting room. The magazine contains many photographs of tractors, detailed stories about old tractors which have done extraordinary things and anecdotes about tractor owners. There are advertisements for second-hand tractors, details of companies which provide tractor tyres and pictures of farmers who have done unusual things with their tractors. It is, not to beat about the bush, the sort of publication which appeals to a rather exclusive readership.

Samuel, as you may have surmised from his reading habits, has a great affection for tractors; an affection which far outweighs his regard for them as utilitarian vehicles. Samuel collects them and, having the space to indulge himself, has a couple of barns full of fine examples of the breed. He claims tax relief on them all on the grounds that he is a farmer buying pieces of farm machinery. It is, he once told me, his ambition to open North Devon's first tractor museum.

This week there was, so it appeared, some sort of problem with the supply of Samuel's favourite reading matter and instead of finding *Tractor Times* on his hall carpet, Samuel found that the delivery boy had pushed a copy of *Angling Weekly* through his letterbox. The magazine contained, as the title rather suggested, a good deal of information, some timely and some historical, about angling. There was nothing at all about tractors in its pages.

Samuel, who has about as much interest in angling as I have in tractors, which is say somewhere between very little and none at all, assumed at first that the delivery boy had made a mistake and that somewhere in the village there must be another one of Peter's customers staring miserably at a copy of *Tractor Times* and wondering what could have happened to his *Angling Weekly*.

So he rang Peter to report the error.

'Oh it wasn't an error,' said Peter merrily. 'The wholesaler didn't have a copy of your magazine so, rather than leave you without something to read, I thought I'd send you a copy of *Angling Weekly*. It was, to be frank, a toss-up between that and *Railway Modeller's Gazette*.

'Why the hell did you think I'd want a magazine about angling?' demanded Samuel rather abruptly.

'Well tractors and fish are both hobbies, aren't they?' replied Peter indignantly.

The fact was, of course, that Peter didn't want to miss the commission on the sale of a magazine and had sent along a replacement more in hope than expectation. However, if he had hoped that Samuel would not bother to return the unwanted magazine he had seriously underestimated Samuel's dislike of wasting money.

According to Thumper, Samuel was not terribly impressed by Peter but it was, said Thumper, not the fact that he had been sent the wrong magazine which had upset him, so much as the fact that Peter had referred to his obsession with tractors as a hobby.

As far as Samuel is concerned, tractors are not a hobby so much as a religion.

We finished loading Cedric's excess manure into Thumper's truck and then went into the house.

'Would you two like a cup of tea?' Patsy asked us. She seemed distracted and rather agitated. Normally Patsy is calm and easy going. She takes most things in her stride. But she definitely wasn't her normal self.

'Can we have one each?' asked Thumper.

Patsy looked at him, puzzled.

I asked her what was worrying her.

'Oh, it's those damned beetles!' she replied suddenly and sharply. 'They're absolutely everywhere. I can't walk around in the kitchen without treading on them. I hate doing that but I can't walk around looking down at the floor all the time. I just trod on another one.

'We'll have to get someone in,' I said. 'I'll ring one of those pest exterminators who advertises in the local paper.'

'Oh I hate the idea of doing that!' said Patsy. 'And he'll want to put poison down everywhere. We can't have that – not with Ben and the cats wandering around the house.'

'Beetle trouble?' said Thumper rather unnecessarily.

'I don't know where they've all come from but we've been invaded by the darned things,' I told him. 'I don't mind one or two but there are dozens and they're all over the place.'

'You need a hedgehog,' said Thumper firmly. 'He'll snuffle and grunt his way round downstairs and get rid of your beetles faster than an exterminator. And you won't need to put any poison down.

Just close the door if you don't want him to go into a particular room.'

'Where on earth am I going to find a hedgehog?'

'There's bound to be one in your garden. They hibernate during the winter but it's a nice sunny day so they'll wake up and have a wander about looking for something to eat. When he's had a nibble, and satisfied his appetite, he'll just go back to sleep again. Just pick one up and bring him into the house for a while. He'll get rid of the beetles for you. Then, when he's done his job, just leave the backdoor open or put him outside again. With all those beetles around you won't need to worry about feeding him.'

'That's a brilliant idea!' said Patsy. 'You two go down the garden and find a hedgehog and I'll put the kettle on – if it isn't full of beetles.'

So Thumper and I tottered down the garden on an impromptu hedgehog hunt.

'I don't know much about hedgehogs,' I confessed as Thumper used a stick to poke carefully at a pile of leaves.

This was something of an understatement. All I knew about hedgehogs was that they were prickly and clearly didn't have much road sense since there were nearly always one or two squashed flat on the lanes in Bilbury. 'What are we looking for? How do we find one?'

'They make very messy nests,' said Thumper. 'There's no real structure to a hedgehog's nest – it will be just a pile of grass, moss and leaves. They're untidy creatures – not very house proud.' He poked at another pile of leaves without any luck. 'Hedgehogs like snuggling into the bottom of bonfires that have been piled up but not lit and you can sometimes find them inside compost heaps.'

'What do they eat?'

'Just about anything you're likely to find crawling about in the garden. Insects of all kinds, slugs, mice and worms. They'll eat baby mice and voles and I've even known one to eat a snake.'

'A snake!' I cried. It seemed unlikely. 'What sort of a snake could a hedgehog eat?'

'Anything that takes their fancy. Grass snakes are usually too big for them but they'll eat an adder if they can find one. They eat it from the tail end and leave the head.'

I was astonished. 'Do they have any predators – apart from cars?'

'Foxes will kill them and eat them if they're hungry enough. A hedgehog will use its muscles to bend its spine and roll itself into a ball if it's threatened but a fox can usually force it open again. If it can't, the fox will roll the spiny ball into a puddle or a pond and that will usually make the hedgehog unroll voluntarily.'

'Clever!'

'Oh, foxes can be very crafty. They know all the survival tricks. Mind you, there are all sorts of old tales about hedgehogs being crafty too. My granddad once told me he'd seen a hedgehog climb up a plum tree, knock off a pile of the plums and then roll over onto the fruit until the plums were impaled on its spike. It would then toddle back to its nest where its partner removes the plums for them both to eat.'

I laughed. 'What a wonderful story! Worthy of Baron Munchausen!'

'My granddad swore it was true,' insisted Thumper. 'And he never had much of an imagination that I know of so it probably was true. He was sober too when he told me that. I've certainly seen a hedgehog climb a tree though it didn't have any plums on it. It was an old stunted oak, with a very bent trunk, easy to climb. The hedgehog climbed up the tree, stayed up there for a while, just having a look around, and then rolled itself into a ball and fell twelve feet to the ground. The spines took the shock and he just walked away. I saw him do it again so he must have enjoyed it.'

All this time Thumper was poking gently at every pile of leaves and moss he could find.

At the far end of our main lawn there is a huge, unusually defined fairy ring; a natural phenomenon which I have always found fascinating.

Because I was frequently embarrassed when visitors who saw our garden wanted to know what caused fairy rings and I couldn't provide any sort of answer other than 'they're some sort of fungus thing, I think' I did a little research into the phenomenon. To start with, I looked at some books in Barnstaple library but in the end, I learned more from our gardener who is a walking encyclopaedia on all garden topics.

Fairy rings are, he told me, caused by a species of fungus and there are three zones. The outer zone is the area of grass into which the fungus is spreading in search of fresh nutrients. Here the grass and other vegetation is stimulated by the action of the fungus on the humus. It is in the middle zone that the fungus is active and here the growth of vegetation is largely suppressed and the grass, therefore, is short and rather unhealthy looking. In the inner zone, the residue left by the dying fungus provides food which enables the grass to grow vigorously. And so you end up with three clear zones – looking like a bull's eye target on a dart board or an archer's target board. The rate at which a fairy ring grows is pretty slow, of course, usually only a few inches a year. Our gardener once told me that he has heard that some fairy rings are hundreds of years old.

Just on the edge of the outer circle of our fairy ring there was another pile of leaves. It looked for all the world as though the leaves had simply been blown there. Thumper had a gentle poke with his stick and the leaves moved. Slowly, a sleepy hedgehog emerged from the pile and looked up at us. He seemed, not unnaturally, to be slightly annoyed at having been woken for no apparent purpose. Anyone would feel the same.

Thumper took off his jacket, an old waxed cotton thing that had seen better days back in the 1950s, and used it to lift the hedgehog up off the grass. He then carried it back to the house while I followed carrying the stick which he'd used to find the hedgehog in the first place.

Once in the kitchen, I shut the back door and Thumper put the hedgehog down on the floor. 'When it's eaten all your beetles just put it back outside where we found it,' he told me.

'Is it a he or a she?' asked Patsy.

Thumper looked at her quizzically. 'Does it matter?'

'I expect it matters to the hedgehog!'

'But not so much to you?'

'No,' agreed Patsy. 'Probably not.'

'You can tell the sex by looking underneath,' said Thumper. 'But to be honest I don't much fancy picking it up to find out. Those prickles are nasty.'

'OK,' said Patsy. 'What shall we call him? We need a name that will do just as well for a girl as for a boy.'

Thumper looked at her as if she were mad.

'Well, if he's going to live with us for a while then he, or she, must have a name,' said Patsy.

'There are lots of names that work for boys or girls,' I pointed out. 'Leslie, Jules, Stevie, Frances, Jamie, Hilary, Adrian, Aubrey, Evelyn as in Evelyn Waugh. There was a male editor of *Punch* magazine called Shirley.' At this point I ran out of steam.

'Let's call it 'Spike',' said Patsy. 'That works either way.'

'I don't believe I'm hearing this!' said Thumper. He looked at Patsy. 'And you a farmer's daughter!'

'It's been all downhill since she married me,' I told him.

'You're not kidding,' replied Thumper. 'You're a bad influence.'

'So, what do we do now?' I asked.

'What do you mean? Take a look at him! Sorry, take a look at her. That's what you wanted isn't it?' He pointed to the hedgehog which was gobbling up a beetle.

'Poor beetle!' murmured Patsy.

'The hedgehog is having his lunch!' cried Thumper.

Just then Ben, our dog, came into the kitchen from the hall. She took one look at the hedgehog, approached gingerly and sniffed. The hedgehog, which had started to earn its keep by finishing off its first beetle with a discernible and slightly unnerving crunching sound, sensed danger and rolled itself into a ball. Ben went closer, caught her nose on one of the hedgehog's spikes and pulled back rapidly. She then stared at the hedgehog and retreated, disappearing back into the hallway.

Thumper drank his tea, ate two home-made cheese scones and left.

By the time he'd gone, the hedgehog had munched its way through an unknown number of beetles. There were already far fewer crawling around on the kitchen floor and it looked very much as though the introduction of the hedgehog was going to be a success.

As indeed it was.

Just over a fortnight later, I gingerly used an old towel to pick up the hedgehog, took it back outside and placed it carefully where Thumper had found it. I picked up a couple of handfuls of dry leaves and sprinkled them over Spike.

He (or she) seemed happy enough for he (or she) didn't move away from where I'd put him (or her) down. There was just some wriggling as he (or she) made himself (or herself) comfortable.

I saw Thumper in the Duck and Puddle that evening and thanked him for finding us a beetle exterminator. I bought him and Patchy a drink and settled down next to the fire. Frank was in the middle of telling a long and rather complicated story which had been told to him, second hand, by the drayman who delivers the beer to the Duck and Puddle.

Apparently another drayman, not the one who had told the story to Frank, had been driving a dray which had collided with a furniture lorry on the narrow, steep road down to Combe Martin. As a result of the collision, a dozen barrels of the brewery's best bitter had rolled off the back of the dray and had rolled down the hill. The drayman had seen them go. None of the barrels had burst open but when another dray arrived to collect them, the two draymen had discovered that every single one of the barrels had a small and surprisingly neat hole through which all of the contents had leaked. Curiously, there was absolutely no sign of any leakage around the barrels for the ground nearby was still firm and baked hard from a week or two of sunshine.

The other odd thing was that three barrels had disappeared completely – never to be found.

Frank said the drayman said he thought something supernatural must have happened. And added that he had always thought that Combe Martin was not the sort of place anyone would want to be after dark.

In the middle of the story, I found myself scratching an itch on my left leg. A few moments later, I had an itch on my right leg. As the story reached its conclusion, I had another itch.

'Have you caught something?' asked Patchy, when I scratched for a third time.

'I don't know what it is,' I confessed. 'Both Patsy and I have been itching and scratching like mad these last few days. I must have picked up a flea from somewhere.'

Suddenly, Thumper started to scratch his arm. And then, a few moments later, he scratched his leg. Then he rubbed his arm again. He looked down, slapped his forearm hard with his other hand and then held up a small creature. He put it onto the palm of his hand. 'Flea!' he said.

The flea, which had been merely dazed by Thumper's blow, leapt away. Patchy and I both jumped away from where we thought it had landed.

'You did sprinkle flea powder onto that hedgehog of yours, didn't you?' said Thumper.

I looked at him. 'Flea powder?'

'You didn't did you?'

'I never thought,' I said. 'You didn't say anything about flea powder.'

'So now it's my fault!' said Thumper.

'No, no. I'm just saying…'

'Well, you've got rid of your beetles and now you've got fleas!' said Thumper. 'You'll have to go home and put flea powder on Ben and your cats. And you'll have to wash all your clothes.'

'Meanwhile, you're barred!' said Frank firmly. 'Drink up and go home.'

I looked at him, open-mouthed. 'Are you serious?'

'You heard me!' said Frank. 'We don't want fleas in here. You're banned.' He looked at me sternly and then started to smile. And then the smile turned into a guffaw.

'Seriously, you'd better go home and have a hot bath,' said Thumper. 'And put your clothes into the washing machine. If you don't, you'll find that all your patients are going to have fleas.'

I left.

Behind me I could hear the three of them laughing at my discomfort.

Friends can be very cruel.

It really was very embarrassing. As I hurried to the car a second flea, or quite possibly a third flea, bit me on the back of my neck.

I found myself wishing we had the beetles back.

Alfie!

I'm sorry to have to call you out,' apologised Carole Singer. She was sitting on the sofa in the living room. She'd left the front door open and I'd just walked in when I'd arrived. Most people in Bilbury don't bother to lock their doors. The door to the living room was shut but when she'd heard me arrive, Mrs Singer had called out to tell me where she was.

'Shut the door, please, doctor,' she said. 'Alfie is around in here somewhere and I don't want him slipping out without my noticing.'

Even lying down her chest was screaming for attention; not for an array of campaign medals or an impressive collection of jewellery but for a cleavage so vast, so endlessly deep, that if I had called down into the depths I would have been able to have a leisurely cup of coffee and a croissant before the echo came bouncing back. I assumed she was wearing some sort of bra designed to boost, promote, exaggerate and advertise. I remembered that Mrs Singer, a villager who could accurately be described as both bustluscious and callipygian, had recently taken up a new profession as a stripper. It seemed as though she was bringing her work home with her.

I didn't know whether Alfie was a cat or a dog but I shut the door as requested.

'I've done something to my ankle. Hopefully I've just sprained it but it hurts so much I'm worried it might be broken,' she said. 'I'm afraid I couldn't walk to Bilbury Grange and I couldn't drive. Gordon would have brought me along to the surgery but he's up in Manchester on business. He's seeing a man in the film industry who is looking for girls to appear in the movies he makes.'

'Congratulations!' I said, for it seemed that congratulations were in order.

'Oh, I know it's not going to be for 'Gone with the Wind' or `The Quiet Man' or one of those big productions. I'm not going to be getting out of a limo in Leicester Square, walking along a red carpet, posing for photographs and waving to crowds.'

She said this as though she thought it might be; just might be. She had a dreamy look in her eyes; full of hope, suddenly alive with dreams that deep down she must have known would never be realised.

'Still it's the movies,' she said, cheerfully. 'And I am excited; even though I expect I'll have to take my clothes off and bounce my boobs a bit. But I do that two or three times a week anyway.' She blushed lightly and lowered her voice. 'Deep down I know the chances are that it will just be to make blue movies and if that's the case then they'll expect me to do more than just take off my clothes. But maybe it will be something better than that.' She paused and brightened up a little. 'And Gordon's excited about it. He said they'd offered to make him an executive producer and might allow him to invest a little of our money in the production.'

It all seemed a bit dodgy to me but I'm not in the business of bursting dreams. I had my doubts about the type of movie the man in Manchester was making but I had to assume that Gordon and Carole, both being considerably over the age of consent, knew what they were contemplating.

'Nothing wrong with hope,' I said. 'Nothing at all.'

'Who am I kidding?' she asked, suddenly deflated. She was speaking to herself as much as to me. 'The title of one of the films is *See Nipples and Die*. It hardly sounds like Oscar winning material, does it?'

I hadn't seen Carole Singer for a while – not since she told me that she was working as a stripper in one or two local public houses. It was a job she had originally begun in order to make ends meet but she had eventually come to terms with the idea of taking off her clothes in public and, I suspect, had actually grown to rather enjoy the attention she received. To her surprise, her husband Gordon hadn't minded when she'd told him where she was going on her evenings out. He'd thought she was attending an exercise class but hadn't been too upset when he'd discovered the nature of the exercise.

She had put on some weight since I'd seen her last.

She was one of those women who seems to be forever putting on weight, dieting and losing it, then putting it back on again. I have a number of patients who have lost 20 stone or more in their lifetime. She now had a definitely Rubenesque look; indeed, she looked as though she had been designed by Peter Paul Rubens on one of his more generous minded days.

She was dressed differently too and the mountainous shires of her bodily kingdom were tightly encased in a figure hugging skirt and a figure hugging jumper.

'How did you hurt your ankle?'

She laughed. 'I fell off a table.'

'Off a table?' I repeated, incredulously. 'What on earth were you doing on a table?'

'Dancing! The landlord thought it would be a good idea if I did my strip while standing on one of the tables in the middle of the pub. He thought the punters would be able to get a better view. So I climbed up onto one of the tables. I'd got my bra off and was just taking off one of my stockings when it happened. There was a puddle of beer on the table that no one had wiped up and on one leg I was a bit wobbly anyway.'

'I would imagine you were,' I said, trying hard not to imagine Mrs Singer, almost naked, standing on one leg in a puddle of beer on a table in the Mott and Bailey or the Gravedigger's Rest.

'Anyway, when I fell, one of the punters half caught me, very kind of him it was too, but I landed a bit funny on the leg which had the stocking half off.'

'And hurt your ankle?'

'Yes. Would you have a look, doctor?' She removed a bag of frozen peas from her ankle and then pulled down and removed her skirt. She tossed it aside in the debonair manner of a practised stripper. She then unfastened the stocking on her left leg, rolled it down and tossed that after the skirt. Underneath the skirt, she was wearing very skimpy, pink, silk panties, a black suspender belt and one remaining stocking.

I examined her ankle. Nothing was broken. 'It's just sprained,' I told her. 'Keep the frozen peas on it, or anything icy, and just rest the leg. Have you got a bandage you could put on?'

'There's one in the bathroom cabinet,' she said.

'Do you want me to fetch it for you?'

'If you don't mind, doctor.'

I popped upstairs to their bathroom, found the bandage and was half way back down the stairs when I came face to face with an

85

adder. Well, more accurately, I came foot to face: my foot and the snake's face.

As is common in many old houses in Bilbury, the Singers have a door at the bottom of their staircase. When I'd gone upstairs I had left the door open.

And there was the adder: half way up, or down, the stairs.

The stair carpet had a pattern on it and the snake was almost invisible.

Almost invisible, but not entirely.

I froze. I have never been over-fond of snakes.

He stuck his tongue out at me, which I thought was rather rude since we'd only just met.

'There's a snake on your stairs!' I called.

'Oh, sorry,' Mrs Singer called back. 'That'll be Alfie I expect.'

'Alfie?'

'My snake.'

'Your snake?'

'I wanted a snake for my act. Lots of the girls use snakes. I don't know why but people find them sexy. You let the snake wind itself round you as you dance.'

'But this is an adder!'

'No, it's just a grass snake. I couldn't afford a snake from a pet shop. Have you any idea what they charge for a snake these days? So Gordon went onto the moor and found me a grass snake. It's a bit small but I'm hoping it will grow.'

I started to say something but Carole hadn't finished.

'It's funny how things change,' she said. 'When Gordon and I got married we were both virgins. We didn't know what we'd got until we got to the hotel after the wedding and unwrapped each other. Now, here's me thinking nothing of dancing round in public, stark naked. And now I'm planning to do it with a snake wrapped round me.' She laughed.

'What made Gordon think this was a grass snake?'

'Oh I don't know. He just picked up the first snake he found. Aren't all the snakes round here called grass snakes?'

'Grass snakes have yellow and black markings round their necks,' I told her. I was still standing on the stairs. The adder was still staring at me. 'And this one isn't going to grow much more because I think it's already pretty well fully grown.'

'You really think it's an adder? Aren't they poisonous?'

'It's definitely an adder. It's a female. And it's poisonous. And it's curled up nice and comfortably on your stair carpet.'

'Oh my God! Oh my God! What are we going to do? How do you know it's female?'

'Because it's light brown and has a dark brown zig zag stripe. The males are grey with a black stripe. Grass snakes are a sort of greeny olive colour. You have to believe me when I tell you that this is definitely not a grass snake.'

'Oh that fool Gordon. It could have bitten me. I could have died. If I hadn't been laid up with my ankle I would have been practising with it.'

'Has it bitten you?'

'No. I haven't been near it. Gordon brought it in before he went off this morning and he let it out so that it could get used to the house – and to me.'

'Your sprained ankle has saved you from a nasty bite.'

'It could have killed me!'

'Adder bites don't usually kill but it wouldn't be very nice to be bitten by one.'

'What are we going to do?'

I peered at the snake. 'It now seems to have gone to sleep on the stairs,' I told her. 'Do you have a telephone in your bedroom?'

'No, I'm afraid not.'

'That's a pity,' I said. 'I was hoping I could ring someone to come and catch it.'

'You could climb out of our bedroom, onto the porch roof,' said Mrs Singer. 'And then you could climb down off the porch roof.'

'OK,' I said. 'I'll try that. Can you hop to the door at the bottom of the stairs and shut it?'

'Oh yes!' she said. I got the impression that she would have happily hopped out of the house and half way to Barnstaple if it had kept her away from the adder.

I waited until I saw the door close. There was no space underneath for the snake to wriggle back down into the living room. I then made my way upstairs, found the Singers' bedroom and climbed out onto the flat roof of the porch. I then jumped down onto their lawn. As I did so, I sprained my ankle slightly. I hobbled back into the house.

'What are we going to do?' demanded Mrs Singer. She was standing on one leg, holding onto the back of a chair to stop herself toppling over.

'I'll ring Thumper Robinson,' I told her. 'May I use your phone?'

'Of course!'

I rang the Duck and Puddle and asked Frank if Thumper was there. He was. I explained that Mrs Singer had an adder on her staircase and asked him if he could come over and rescue it, and us. He said he would be with us in a couple of minutes. It felt good knowing that Thumper was on his way. Thumper is the sort of man who will walk across a field full of cows without looking about him nervously, breaking into a cold sweat or imperceptibly increasing his pace so as to get to the other side of the field before one of the cows becomes aggressive or, worse still, turns into a bull. While we waited, I thought I might as well do something useful so I put the bandage on Mrs Singer's ankle.

'It's on the stairs,' I told Thumper when he arrived. He had with him a forked stick, a sack and a broom handle to which was attached a wire loop. He explained that the idea was to put the loop around the snake and to lift it into the air so that it would have no firm foundation if it decided to strike. Thumper was wearing a pair of thick gauntlets – the sort which used to be favoured by motorcyclists in the 1950s but which went out of favour for some reason. I didn't blame him at all. I wouldn't tackle a poisonous snake unless I was wearing armour. He looked at me and then at Mrs Singer. She still hadn't got round to putting her skirt back on.

'Hello, Carole!' he said. Carole simpered rather coyly.

'Mrs Singer has sprained her ankle,' I explained.

'Sorry to hear it,' said Thumper. He cautiously opened the door at the bottom of the stairs and two minutes later, he had the snake in the sack.

'I'll release it on the moor,' he said to Mrs Singer. 'I assume you don't want to keep it?'

'Oh no, please take it! Get rid of it!' said Mrs Singer without hesitation. 'But don't hurt it!' she added.

'I'd better be off,' I said, when Thumper had gone. I looked at my watch. My evening surgery was due to start in ten minutes time. 'You haven't got any more snakes around the place, have you?'

'No,' said Mrs Singer, laughing rather nervously.

I hobbled to the car.

'Oh doctor,' called Mrs Singer who had followed me to the front door. 'Could I have a sick note for the pub? I don't think I'll be able to strip for a couple of days.'

I went back and wrote out a sick note. She was still not wearing her skirt. 'And when you do go back to work it might be a good idea to keep off slippery tables,' I told her.

When I'd done that I headed back to the car.

'Hello!' said Patsy when I got back home. 'You seem to have had a busy afternoon!'

'Don't ask,' I said.

'I don't need to,' she said. 'Mrs Rathbone called to let me know that she saw you climbing out of the Singers' bedroom window and then ten or fifteen minutes later she saw you and Mrs Singer standing on the doorstep.'

'Yes,' I said.

'She said Mrs Singer wasn't wearing a skirt and had only one stocking on.'

'She's sprained her ankle.'

'Why are you limping?'

'I sprained an ankle when I climbed out of the bedroom window.'

'Golly! Is it catching?'

'I've just got time for a cup of tea and a biscuit before surgery starts,' I said wearily. 'I'll tell you about it later. Believe me, I've had a tough time.'

'It sounds as if you have,' said Patsy with a grin. 'I can't wait to hear all about it. The bit about you climbing out of the bedroom window should be particularly worth hearing.'

The Man in the Hat

I had, over the years, seen Dyfed Steele a good many times.

He wasn't Welsh, though his Christian name sounded more Welsh than English.

He had, so he once told me, been conceived while his parents were on their honeymoon in Port Talbot. He didn't know if there was any significance to the choice of the name Dyfed, but he said his mother had seen the name on a lorry and had rather liked it; thinking it stylish, manly and a little different.

Apart from having a slightly less than usual Christian name, the most immediately notable oddity about Dyfed was that he always wore a hat. He wore it outdoors and indoors. He wore it while eating and he wore it when sitting in my consulting room. It was a flat cap, a piece of headgear that had definitely seen better days, and I don't think he ever took it off. There were rumours that he wore it when he took his bi-monthly bath and rumours that he wore it in bed. There were some in the village who wondered whether anyone, including his lady wife, had ever seen the top of his head at all.

Dyfed lived in a small, red brick two up and two down which had once been a farm labourer's tied cottage and he had lived there for as long as I could remember, sharing the house with his wife, a normally pleasant, friendly woman called Emily.

The two of them used to row a good deal and occasionally china would be thrown, though usually, I am pleased to say, with more passion than accuracy. He once came to me with a nasty bruise on his right cheek, apparently from a flying cup, and she once had a slight cut and a bruise on her shoulder from a tea plate which had shattered on impact. The arguments never lasted very long, however.

Mrs Kennet, Patsy's mother knew them well and said that the two of them 'always buried the hatchet quickly but always dug it up again before the day was out'.

Emily, who was not the brightest bulb in the chandelier, was the most enthusiastic slimmer I can remember ever meeting. Both she and Dyfed had been on diets ever since I'd known them and I once noted that according to the medical records I collected, Emily had, over the years, lost a total of 2,200 pounds.

As a general rule, they each weighed somewhere between 250 and 300 pounds.

That means that whether you measured them in Imperial tons, American tons or Metric tons, they weighed around a quarter of a ton together. (What a wonderful tribute to diversity it is that a simple word like 'ton' should mean so many very different things according to where it is measured.)

As Thumper once said, it was a good job the Steeles didn't ride a tandem bicycle together.

Dyfed Steele was one of those patients who seem to be a trifle unlucky and his weight didn't seem to help his luck.

Take, for example, what happened in the depths of a winter when most of Bilbury was covered in a foot of snow and the parts that didn't have a foot of snow were covered in drifts several feet deep.

The snow fell so consistently and so heavily that every morning I had to traipse around the garden at Bilbury Grange, knocking the snow off our trees and bushes so that the weight of it didn't break the branches. It is, of course, the evergreens which suffer most; their larger surface area means that the weight of snow on them can be extraordinary.

The house itself was festooned with icicles, which the locals call frost candles, and when moving in and out of the house we kept a watchful eye on the icicles above us. It is no fun to be speared by a falling icicle. A few years earlier a man the other side of Bideford had been killed by an icicle which had landed on his neck and cut through his spine and spinal cord. It never fails to surprise me just how many strange ways there are for men to die.

Now, there is in Bilbury one particular pond which is always popular with ice skaters.

The pond (it would be exaggerating its size and importance to call it a lake though many in the village refer to it as such) is just west of Softly's Bottom and doesn't cover much more than a third of an acre in total.

As a general rule, locals usually regard three inches of clear black ice as safe for skating. More is better. Less is risky. When the ice is clear and fairly thick then it can be safe even if cracking can be heard and cracks can be seen.

Much less ice than three inches is suicidal.

If the ice isn't black and seems to contain snow, then even twice that thickness isn't enough.

Of course, the risk also depends very much upon the nature of the water underneath the ice. If the water is shallow then the biggest risk is that any skaters who go through will get a soaking. But if the water is deeper and fast flowing, with a noticeable current, then the risks can be very serious. The most dangerous situation is a river which has fast running water in the middle and slow running water at the sides. The danger is that whereas the ice at the edges of the river seems solid and safe, the ice in the middle may be very thin and a skater who goes through there may be swept along by the current and unable to escape from their icy roofed grave.

And, of course, everything changes if a bunch of people are skating – especially if they keep close together.

Well, during the winter about which I am writing, a dozen people had been happily skating on the pond, with nothing untoward happening, when Dyfed saw the fun they were having. Not unnaturally, he decided that he wanted to join in. So he borrowed a pair of skates.

And within three minutes he had gone through the ice and was standing up to his waist in cold water.

The problem, of course, was getting him out of the pond.

Dyfed didn't have the upper body strength to raise himself up out of the water and no one else could possibly lift him. Attempts to pull him out of the pond failed miserably when poor Dyfed complained that he was being pulled into the raw ice edge of the hole he'd made.

In the end, the only way to rescue him was to break a path in the ice all the way through to the point where Dyfed had gone through. Once this had been done, Dyfed was able to wade to the shore, safety and the blanket being held by the ever faithful Emily.

Unfortunately, to make things worse for Dyfed, a reporter from the local paper happened to be present and his adventures found their way onto page three of the next week's issue.

'Too Much Weight –Too Little Ice!' was the headline.

Dyfed was more than a little unpopular with those who had wanted to carry on skating for it took another few days for the ice to repair itself sufficiently for more skating. Not surprisingly, Dyfed was banned from going onto the ice any more.

I suppose you could say that the ice skating thing could have been put down to a lack of insight, or a lack of common sense, but if strange things were going to happen then they tended to happen to Dyfed.

The truth was that the only sort of luck he ever had was bad luck. If he had ever won the lottery he would have lost the ticket.

Whenever I saw him, I was reminded of Dante Alighieri, the woeful Italian poet who was one of the first package tourists in history and who in his Divine Comedy described how he went on a guided tour through the nine circles of hell.

I sometimes thought that Dyfed had set out on his own version of Dante's endless trial. He was always in and out of my surgery, invariably with something out of the ordinary to report.

Take the bees, for example.

Now, quite a few people in Bilbury keep bees. I can, off the top of my head, think of half a dozen keen apiarists within two miles of Bilbury Grange. Like all the others, Dyfed kept bees and collected his own honey. It was splendid stuff too for their garden, whence from the bees collected their pollen, was well stocked with a wide variety of clovers, the sort of plants which honey connoisseurs claim produces the finest tasting honeys.

Dyfed told me that David, the chap with the sling who had beaten Goliath in single combat, had reported that he had found, when pursuing the Philistines, that honey was the original 'super food' in that it revived, restored, healed and invigorated. David should have known for few people needed more reviving, restoring, healing or invigorating.

But Dyfed was the only bee keeper I knew who was regularly stung by his bees.

Most of those who keep bees seemed to develop some sort of rapport with their swarms. Even though they are, technically at least, stealing the honey the bees have made, they manage to build up something approaching a relationship.

They took the honey, it was true, but they took it as a sort of rent on the fine properties and sense of security they provided in the form of well-made and well looked after hives.

Most of the apiarists I knew did not even bother to wear the usual protective clothing favoured by beekeepers. I thought them quite mad, and braver than I could ever be, but they didn't often get stung.

Dyfed, on the other hand, did not have any sort of relationship with his bees.

Or rather, I suppose he did have a relationship but it was distinctly and exclusively antagonistic.

When collecting honey, he wore all the gear: the hood with see-through facemask, the one-piece suit, the thick gauntlets and the boots. Wandering down the garden path, he looked for all the world as though he had just landed from Mars and was hunting around for a suitable decompression chamber. You would not have thought it possible that anything could have snuck into that suit. And underneath the beekeeper's guard he wore a long-sleeved, woollen vest and long-legged, woollen underpants – the sort favoured and heartily recommended by men and women who climb Everest or explore the icy wastes of the Arctic or Antarctic. On warm days he must have been roasting. But still the bees managed to sting him. Every pound of honey he collected resulted in half a dozen stings and he would come in from the garden, make sure all the doors and windows were shut, strip off and sit in a kitchen chair for half an hour while Emily, armed with the pair of tweezers Dyfed had used to handle his stamps when he was a boy, and had a fine collection of British Commonwealth Commemoratives, would gently remove the stings which the hapless bees had left behind. It always seemed to me to be a rather high price to pay for a pound or so of honey.

And then there was the whisky still.

I really don't know what possessed him to set up a whisky still. He wasn't a heavy drinker. He had no intention of selling the stuff he made. And for the money he spent on equipment, he could have bought himself a case of good malt whisky. I sometimes think he just started the still to see what would happen; to see whether he could get away with it.

As far as I understand it (and I am no expert) you need several things to make a whisky still.

First, you need a pile of potatoes which are surplus to normal requirements, or some grain that has started to sprout. This is the 'whatever'.

Before it can be turned into something drinkable (and probably toxic) the 'whatever' you choose to use has to be mixed with loads of hot water, stirred a good deal and then filtered.

And then you need something with which you can heat the liquid from which you intend to obtain the alcohol, something else to help the vapour condense before it escapes and disappears, and another something else that will cool and then trap the alcohol you hope you have produced.

And you also need a thermometer.

It is, as you can see, a good deal more complicated than just wandering into the Duck and Puddle and asking Frank to pour you a snifter.

Now most people who set up illicit stills (and I don't think even Dyfed was ignorant of the fact that it is illegal to make your own alcohol) put together all the bits and pieces they need from stuff they have lying around the house or in a shed. Or they collect the necessary impedimenta a bit at a time so that no one supplier knows precisely what they are doing. I assume that burglars follow the same basic principle: buy the sack with 'swag' written on it from one supplier, the mask for disguising one's appearance from a second, the striped jumper from a third and the jemmy from a fourth. Only a fool would choose to buy all four items from same emporium.

This was not the way for Dyfed.

He had a glut of King Edward potatoes one year and after deciding that he might try his hand at converting the excess into something more useful than chips, mash and jacket potatoes he sent off for a Home Distillation Kit which he saw advertised in one of those funny little underground magazines that were so popular in the late 1960s and early 1970s.

And, you will not be terribly surprised to hear that he had hardly finished unpacking the kit before there was a knock on his front door and a bunch of policemen stormed in and arrested him. This was the most exciting thing to have happened to the police of North Devon in a generation or more and they weren't about to miss the opportunity to get their man banged to rights.

At this point, Dyfed did have an unusual stroke of luck in that the policemen who had burst through his front door had moved a little too eagerly. And because Dyfed hadn't even unpacked the bits and pieces he'd bought, let alone put it all together, let alone found out what he was supposed to do, let alone actually manufactured anything illicit, there wasn't much of a case for the prosecution to get their teeth into. Dyfed could, I suppose, have claimed that he just wanted to see what the equipment looked like. He could have argued that he had ordered the stuff by mistake.

You can arrest people for all sorts of strange things but the prosecution decided in the end that you really can't expect to convict someone for being in possession of a pressure cooker and a few bits of tubing and glassware.

The other bit of good fortune Dyfed had lay in the fact that the supplier had forgotten to include the instruction booklet which had supposed to be a part of the package. In the end, the authorities had to let him go with a stern warning. But they nevertheless confiscated all the stuff he'd bought – on the dubious grounds that they could.

That was the whisky still fiasco.

And, of course, there was the time that Dyfed, who was old enough to know better, decided to emulate Evil Knievel, an American stunt rider who was at the time very famous for riding his motorcycle over rows of double decker buses and who a year or two later tried to jump the Grand Canyon on some sort of crazy motorcycle fitted with wings.

Several local boys had injured themselves trying to do tricks on their bicycles.

Two, I remember, had arranged a couple of planks, a packing case and a variety of other bits of waste wood in an attempt to create a stunt scenario of their own. They had persuaded a young sister to lie down at the end of the ramp they'd made and it was more by the grace of God than through any skill that they both managed to miss her. Indeed, it was their complete lack of skill which saved the girl because they both fell off the plank before they could do the leap they had hoped to execute. One had a sprained ankle and a bruised knee and the other knocked out two milk teeth which were about ready to come out anyway.

None of the children who hurt themselves did anything which a little Dettol and some sticking plaster couldn't put right.

But Dyfed, of course, had to have a go at being Evil Knievel.

He was well into his 30s at the time, the age at which a man can reasonably be expected to be at least on nodding terms with maturity.

Not owning, or having access to, a motorbike, Dyfed was forced to use a pedal cycle for his record breaking attempt. And, to make things worse, the bike he chose to use, because it was the only one in the Steele household, was an old sit up and beg machine which belonged to his wife and which was equipped with one of those neat, little woven baskets fitted to the front handlebars.

Unlike the young boys who had tried a similar exploit, Dyfed did not build himself a ramp. Oh no. Nothing so rational would do for Dyfed. Instead, he chose to attempt to leap over a local stream by riding the borrowed bicycle as fast as he could across a field. He turned his hat back to front, so that the peak lay behind him and would not slow him down, and he made his attempt with an audience of one: the long suffering Emily.

Predictably, the attempt proved to be quite beyond his skills and the machine's capabilities. When the bicycle, with Dyfed on board, reached the nearside bank, it had failed to attain sufficient speed to enable it to become airborne. It is, perhaps, important to remember that at the time of the accident, Dyfed weighed considerably in excess of his usual 250 pounds. And he wasn't fit enough to peddle a bicycle at a decent speed on the rough ground of a grassy field. So, instead of flying through the air with the greatest of ease, the bicycle merely plunged front wheel first into the stream, throwing the hapless rider into the mud of the opposite bank.

It could have been worse. It could have been much worse.

As it was, Dyfed broke his collarbone, cut his hand and suffered a number of stings from the bed of nettles into which he crashed. The bicycle, which was even less fortunate than its rider, landed on a rather large stone, and ended up with a buckled front wheel. It now resides with an old iron bedstead and a retired mangle at the bottom of the Steele's garden.

It was the evening when Dyfed came to the surgery to have the stitches removed from his hand that I finally plucked up the courage to seek the answer to the question I had harboured since the ambulance had taken him off to the hospital.

'I hope you don't think it rude of me to ask,' I said as I carefully removed the first of the stitches, 'but did you take your cap off at the hospital?'

'They wanted me to,' he said.

'But did you?'

'Certainly not.'

'Why not?' I asked.

It was probably impertinent but I was, I confess, curious to know why he wouldn't remove the damned hat. I confess I had wondered if it could simply be that he was bald, or balding, and embarrassed about his hairless pate. There was, however, plenty of hair poking out at the sides and the back of the hat so I knew he was not entirely bald.

'It's embarrassing,' said Dyfed, going slightly red.

'I'm not going to find it embarrassing,' I told him. 'And it might be something I can help you with.'

He thought about it for a while while I continued to snip away and remove the stitches in his hand.

'Would you draw the curtains, please?'

'Draw the curtains?'

'Yes, please. But don't put on the light.'

I removed the last stitch. Everything looked clean and healthy. I then drew the curtains.

'There you are,' said Dyfed, removing his cap.

The top of his head was surprisingly bald and sitting in the middle of his scalp was a lump about an inch high and an inch wide.

'Can I put my hat back on, now?'

'No, no, wait a moment. Let me look at it, first.'

'Be quick then, doctor.'

I examined the lump. It was a fairly ordinary cyst.

'I have to put my hat back on,' said Dyfed. He seemed quite distressed.

'Why?' I asked him. 'Why do you need to put your hat back on so quickly?'

'Because if the light gets to it then it will turn cancerous and I'll have to have the top of my head taken off.'

'It's a perfectly harmless lump,' I told him. 'You could shine a light on it all day and it wouldn't turn cancerous. Who told you that nonsense?'

'Mrs Hathaway.'

'Who is Mrs Hathaway?'

'The woman who lives next door but one to my aunt Brenda.'

'Where does your aunt Brenda live?'

'In Giggleswade.'

'Has Mrs Hathaway seen your lump?'

'No. But Emily described it to my aunt Brenda on the telephone. And my aunt Brenda then told Mrs Hathaway. And Mrs Hathaway said that it was pre-cancerous and that I should keep it out of the light and away from the air as much as possible.'

'So you keep your hat on?'

'It seemed the best thing to do.'

'When was this?'

'Six years ago.'

'Well she was talking rubbish,' I told him. 'And that's why you have been wearing your hat all these years?'

'Yes. And it hasn't turned into cancer, has it?'

'No. And it hasn't and won't. It's just an ordinary lump: a lipoma.'

'A what?'

'A lipoma. It's just a fatty lump. It won't do you any harm. They don't usually develop on the head but there it is, it has.'

Dyfed looked at me doubtfully. 'You mean it really won't hurt for the sunshine to get on it?'

'No. Do you want it removed?'

'Removed?'

'Taken away?'

'Can you do that?'

'Certainly.'

'And it would disappear completely?'

'Just a little scar to show where it had been.'

'I'd need to go to the hospital wouldn't I?'

'If you want to go to the hospital I could make an appointment for you to see a surgeon. But there are long waiting lists in the NHS these days. He'll see you in three or four months' time for a preliminary consultation. And then he'll put you on the waiting list and eventually, if you're lucky, he'll remove the lump in another twelve or eighteen months' time. You won't get it done much sooner because it's not life threatening in any way. If you're lucky, you could probably have it removed in just under two years – that's if all goes well and the waiting lists don't grow any longer.'

'Oh.'

Now that he had found out that he could have the lump removed, Dyfed sounded disappointed at the prospect of having to wait so long.

'Or you could take your jacket off, lie down on the couch and let me remove it now.'

'You can take it off?' said Dyfed. He sounded startled; as though I'd offered to shine his shoes or change his sparking plugs.

'Of course. It's a small lump and I'm a doctor and you're my last patient.'

'But you said it would take the hospital two years to take it off.'

'It probably would. But I'm quicker than them. I could take it off in a quarter of an hour.'

'Do you do things like this?'

'I do,' I told him. 'I did a few of them when I worked as a house surgeon.' I took my Swiss Army penknife out of my pocket and opened the largest blade. 'This should be plenty big enough.'

Dyfed looked at me with terror in his eyes.

'Just kidding,' I told him, putting the penknife back into my pocket. 'I've got a proper scalpel and some anaesthetic stuff I can inject so that you don't feel a thing.'

And so three minutes later Dyfed was lying on my examination couch with his head positioned so that I could get at his scalp.

I cleaned the whole area, wiped it down with a strong antiseptic solution, and then injected a local anaesthetic into the skin all around the lipoma.

Five minutes after that I started work removing the lipoma.

Less than twenty minutes later, I was sewing up the wound I'd made and Dyfed Steele no longer had a lipoma sitting in the middle of his largely bald head.

When I'd finished I was, to be frank, quite proud of the job I'd made. It had been a year or two since I'd removed a lump that big. I taped a dressing over the stitches where the lump had been.

'You'll have to come back and see me to have these new stitches removed,' I told him. 'But come back tomorrow and let me have a look at it so that I can change the dressing.'

It occurred to me that it was rather surreal that he should come into the surgery to have one lot of stitches removed and leave with a fresh lot in a different part of his body.

'Can I put my hat on now, doctor?' asked Dyfed.

I stared at him, disbelievingly. 'You don't have to wear your hat now.'

'Oh, I think I'll keep it on, if you don't mind, doctor,' said Dyfed. 'It would feel odd not to be wearing my hat. Besides, when my missus last saw my head, there was more hair on it.'

'So are you just going to keep the hat on all the time?'

'Oh, yes, I think so.'

I might as well have left the damned lump where it was. It hadn't been doing any harm.

Gwladys Gwilliams

Gwladys Gwilliams, who was well into her 80s when I first met her, lived in a small house by the river. She lived with Bobby, a small dog of an indeterminate make whom she loved very much. She was an elegant, noticeable and easily remembered woman. She always wore make-up, meticulously applied. Her hair was always neatly done. She always dressed smartly. And a charming smile was never far from her lips. I had no doubt, that she had once been both toothsome and eesome.

She once explained to me that her parents had christened her Gwladys (which was, apparently, a common spelling variation at the time of her birth) and that she had later paid a few pounds to a solicitor who had arranged to have her surname adjusted to match. She said she was in show business at the time and felt that a catchy name might help her move up the ladder a little easier. Unfortunately, it didn't.

Miss Gwilliams's home was called River Cottage. It was a very small house which had just two rooms upstairs and two downstairs. It was just over a 100-years-old but it was still one of the youngest properties in the village.

When the last cottage had been finished in the 19th century, and the last builder had fitted the last slate in position, it seems to have been decided that that was that; that Bilbury was pretty much complete, in the same way that a suit of clothes is complete when the last button has been sewn into place.

There had, of course, been a number of attempts to extend the size of the village and not a few individuals had applied for permission to build a house here, a house there. Most of the applications had been rejected. Attempts to build housing estates had been defeated.

Since the house in which Miss Gwilliams lived was known to get flooded almost every winter, she paid a very modest peppercorn rent to live there.

The owners, who lived in London, had bought the house in the summer a few years earlier and had not realised that their new holiday home would be flooded during the colder, wetter months. I don't think anyone actually lied to them. I just don't think they were sensible enough to ask the right questions. The river, boosted by rain from the nearby hills, brought down by dozens of tiny tributaries, invariably burst its banks in November and the ground floor of the house would stay wet, if not completely under water, until late March.

There wasn't a good deal of sympathy for the owners in the village.

'You would have thought,' said Patchy Fogg, 'that they would have seen the high water mark, two foot six inches above the top of the skirting boards in all the rooms downstairs.'

The Londoners had tried to sell the house but no one else had been daft enough to want to buy it. They didn't want to use it themselves because the first flood had not only destroyed their lovely rugs, their smart, new television set and their kitchen equipment but it had also broken their hearts. They couldn't bear to return to the site of their Great Mistake.

In the end, they allowed a local estate agent to offer it as a rental property. After being on the market, and empty, for nine months, the agent managed to rent out the property to Miss Gwilliams on the understanding that she would be responsible for all the local taxes and for some basic maintenance. In addition, she paid just £20 a year as a peppercorn rent and she had an agreement that gave her the right to live in the property for as long as she liked. The owners, tired of their North Devon cottage, had effectively washed their hands of it and considered themselves lucky to be free of the associated responsibilities and liabilities.

Miss Gwilliams didn't mind that her house flooded.

She got round the problem by ignoring the ground floor completely. She hired Thumper Robinson to put up a small partition on the top floor and with this he divided one of the two rooms into a tiny bathroom and a tiny kitchen. Thumper installed a sink, a bath and a lavatory in the bathroom and a cooker and a couple of old cupboards in the kitchen.

The other upstairs room she used as a bed-sitting room. Every surface in that room was covered with photographs of her. In some of the pictures she was alone, dressed in costumes – most of which were revealing. In some of the photographs she was in a group or with another performer – some of them very famous. There was one photograph of her sitting on Peter Sellers' lap. She had an arm around his neck and was wearing nothing but a feather in her hair. He was wearing a suit and was pretending to be startled; somehow surprised to find that he had a naked girl on his knees.

The cottage was, in truth, all very cosy.

Miss Gwilliams had all the downstairs electrics disconnected and bought herself a decent pair of fisherman's waders.

If the river water came into the house for the winter well, it would go away again, wouldn't it?

'It's not as if it's sewage or drain water,' she said. 'It doesn't smell or leave anything nasty behind. I get a bit of weed left downstairs and once I found a dead trout stuck in the fireplace. But the water level never goes up too high for my waders.'

No one else wanted to be a tenant of River Cottage but maybe that was because no one else had the imagination to see that by turning the cottage into a home on stilts it would become a quite desirable property.

For a very modest outlay, Miss Gwilliams had turned an unwanted property into the home of her dreams. She had a splendid view up and down the river and marvellous views across the moors to the East.

In her youth, Miss Gwilliams had performed in various revue bars in London and had been a member of a variety troupe which had travelled around the country performing in provincial theatres and music halls.

She didn't have many visitors and whenever I saw her she always told me a little more about her life.

'Maybe you'll write about me in one of your books,' she once said. 'I'd like that.'

Bit by bit I learned about her extraordinary experiences.

She had spent her early and middle years on the fringes of show business and now she lived as much in her memories as in the world around her.

As my friend Will once put it, talking about someone else, 'she spoke about her vicissitudes with veritable and verifiable verisimilitude'.

People sometimes sneer at older folk for living in the past but it has always seemed to me that we belittle our lives if we forget the past and, besides, hers were remembrances rather than longings. Even the young will look at a photo album or a souvenir with affection.

In most decent lives, the regrets of omission (the list of things we could and should have done but didn't do) far outweigh the regrets of commission (the things we did do but need not have done and should not have done) and Miss Gwilliams was no exception. From time to time, as she told me of her life she would halt and look away for a moment or two. When she looked back I could see moistness in her eyes and I knew the tears were there because of a disappointment remembered or an opportunity missed.

I visited her regularly because after she came to Devon she developed bronchitis and emphysema. I don't think the damp helped. Living by a river can be especially bad for you if you have problems with your lungs. And it doesn't help, of course, if the river has a habit of coming indoors for a while during the winter months.

The chest problems were the most serious of her health troubles but she had, over the years, managed to collect quite a library of ailments. She used to ask me to visit a bit more often than was really necessary and I think she was probably just lonely.

If she asked for a visit in the winter when her house was flooded, she would sometimes ask me to take her a basket of shopping from Peter Marshall's shop. She always insisted on paying me for the groceries. When I visited her between November and March, I always put a pair of fisherman's waders in the boot of the Rolls Royce.

It was Miss Gwilliams who taught me the art of dunking a biscuit.

When she gave me a cup of tea she always produced a plateful of biscuits.

'Dunk if you like, doctor,' she said one day.

I picked up a bourbon cream and dipped it into my tea.

'Oh no, no, doctor!' she said, laughing and waving a finger in mock admonishment. 'You're doing it all wrong.'

She explained that there is quite an art, and a bit of science maybe, to dunking a biscuit properly.

For a start, there's the choice of the biscuit. Speciality items such as custard creams and bourbons aren't the best for dunking. Digestive and rich tea biscuits are more suitable.

Next, you must be careful not to put too much biscuit into the tea.

'Between half an inch and three quarters of an inch is plenty,' she said. 'And then, when you've dunked, you should quietly count 'one, two' before withdrawing. If you put a biscuit in too far, or leave it submerged for too long, it will become soggy and break and that's disastrous!'

She told me that she had it on the very best authority that Queen Elizabeth II was a secret dunker. ('A friend of mine has a daughter who works at the Palace. She insists she's often seen the Queen dunking the royal biscuit.)

She also said that Cary Grant was a keen dunker. 'I knew him when he was known as Archie Leach and working in vaudeville. He was an acrobatic dancer but also a very funny man. He toured the same music halls that I did for a while. He didn't emigrate to America until later.'

I promised her that I would tell her story in one of my books about the village of Bilbury and the people who live there.

Miss Gwilliams was, I think a romantic. Romantics always find failure much easier to cope with than success. And although no one could say that her career was a great success, there is absolutely no doubt that Miss Gwilliams enjoyed her life in show business.

She told me that she had, at various times, been a singer ('I wasn't terribly good but I wore a rather daring gown and so I got away with it), a magician's assistant ('He was called The Great something or other and he used to cut me in half every night, and twice on Wednesdays and Saturdays, but I left that job when he started to drink and nearly did cut me in half one night.'), a juggler's assistant ('He was lovely. He was Italian and I thought I'd found true love. Unfortunately, he wasn't a terribly good juggler and he wasn't a terribly good boyfriend. He was fired and ran back to Italy with a toffee-nosed soprano who was at least twice his age and six inches taller than him. I don't mean to be catty but I'd still scratch her eyes out if I saw her now.')

And she became the girl who looked after the costumes and the props and she made herself indispensable by making endless cups of tea and fetching packets of fish and chips at the end of each show.

When the Windmill Theatre opened in London, Miss Gwilliams became one of the famous nude models in the 'tableaux vivants'.

'I was older than all the other girls and some of them knew that and they treated me like a mum. I was more experienced than any of them because I'd been on tour around the music halls. I'd been in show business for years and I knew how things worked. I'd worked with some big music hall stars.'

'I told the management that I was 29 but I was 12 years older than that. Fortunately, I'd kept my figure and I've always had good skin and they believed me. I'd learned how to do really good make-up from a lady I worked with on the music halls. Her name was Kate Carney and she was hugely successful. She had a huge eleven bedroom house, expensive cars and race horses. In the 1930s, she used to be accompanied on the piano by a man who was her butler. Well, at least he pretended to be her butler. I don't think anyone really knew for sure. She did three Royal variety shows back in the days when a Royal variety show really meant something. During the Second World War, she was still working and she would often ignore the air raid warnings. She loved being on stage so much that she never wanted to end a show. I've known her carry on with a show until four o'clock in the morning. She's forgotten now but she was a big star in her day and she was very kind to me. It's funny, isn't it? Even the big stars get forgotten as their day goes and their names fade. They think they're immortal but they aren't, of course. You have to be a very special sort of star, a Marie Lloyd, a George Formby or a Stanley Holloway to last after you've died.'

'Actually, when they started with the nude shows I think the Windmill had a bit of a job finding girls who'd perform naked. They wanted actresses; young ladies who could be elegant even without wearing costumes. We had to go onto the stage stark naked and stand perfectly still. We tried to get into a comfortable position that you could hold for as long as possible because we were warned that the show would be closed if we moved. A lovely man called Vivian Van Damm was the manager and he was in charge of creating the nude scenes. He came up with some right corkers. Once, we all had to pretend to be mermaids. Another time we were supposed to be Red Indian squaws with feathers in our hair. The only thing the scenes had in common was that the girls were damned near naked. And the important bits were always on show. If you had long hair you had to keep it off your chest. 'The punters want to see nipples,' said Mr Van Damm.

The Lord Chamberlain, who was in charge of censoring all theatre shows in London, said: 'If you move, it's rude.' So that was that. We didn't move.'

'Later on Mr Van Damm had this idea for a fan dance. One of us would go on stage naked but holding a fan. There would be four other girls, in skimpy costumes, and they would hold fans too. The naked girl would dance about with her body concealed by the five fans. At the end of the dance all the fans would be pulled away revealing the girl's body. She had to stand stock still because the rule was still the same as before: 'If you move, it's rude'.

'One or two of the girls didn't like dancing around nude, usually because they'd acquired boyfriends or fiancés who didn't mind them posing nude if they kept still but didn't approve if they bounced around a bit behind a fan. I never understood that. I never minded being naked and I was very popular. These days I would have been considered too plump but in those days the gentlemen who came to the Windmill liked their girls to have curves in the right places. Gentlemen regularly used to wait for me outside the stage door. Most of them were in town for business. If I liked them, I used to go to dinner with them. If I really liked them and they seemed to be real gentlemen, I'd go back to their hotel with them, though I always had to leave before morning so that the hotel management didn't get upset. The little presents I was given helped me buy my luxuries; nicer frocks, pretty hats and shoes. Some of the gentlemen used to give perfume or bits of jewellery but I always preferred cash. Some of the hotels were a bit sniffy and I had to sneak out the back way through the kitchens.'

'We had all sorts of other tricks to get round the rules about not moving on the stage. We used to sit naked on a swing seat and a couple of girls in costumes would push us. The Lord Chamberlain said that was all right because it was the seat that was moving. Can you imagine anything so daft?'

'In the end, I had to leave the stage because someone told the boss how old I was. I never knew who told on me but I had my suspicions because not many people there knew the truth. Mr Van Damm didn't believe it when he knew my real age. He was in tears when he told me I'd have to go. I think he was frightened people would find out they had a woman my age on the stage. They liked to give the impression the girls were all young and virginal! I'd have gone on there forever if it had been left to me. Still, I had a good run for my money.'

'They let me work there behind the scenes for a while and I was there after the War when Mr Van Damm started hiring young comedians. I remember we had Tony Hancock, Harry Secombe, Peter Sellers, Tommy Cooper, Bruce Forsyth, Arthur English, Michael Bentine and Jimmy Edwards working there. They were all lovely young lads. I remember more than one or two of them liked watching the girls from the wings but Jimmy Edwards wasn't so interested. We didn't find out until later why that might have been, bless him. Peter Sellers was my favourite. He was a lovely man. Michael Bentine was funny. Tommy Cooper was nervous to start with but I knew he was going to be a star. He worked harder than some people thought. But they were all lovely. I thought of them as my lovely boys.'

'But then there was a bit of a fuss with the police. I got into trouble for talking to a gentleman outside the stage door. I thought he wanted to be friendlier than he wanted to be and he turned out to be a spoilsport and a sneak. He called a policeman who arrested me. Then I lost my job completely.'

'I found myself a little room in Soho and earned a living giving French lessons. I was the first to think that one up. I had a little card pinned up in a newsagent's shop in Wardour Street. Sometimes I used to get people come up really wanting French lessons. I used to tell them I was full up with students and send them away. I also had a card up for a while that said 'Chest for sale'. That was another girl's idea and it didn't work as well as the French lessons card. I used to pay the newsagent £1 a month to have my card in his window but then I found I didn't really need it. I just thumb-tacked a small advertisement next to the bell where I was living There were six girls living in the building and there were six adverts tacked next to the six bells.'

'And then I met Lionel. He was a lovely man. He was a cobbler who had a little shop just off Wardour Street. He'd inherited the shop from his father. It had been in the family for three generations. He worked really hard and he could do anything with shoes and boots. However badly they were worn, he could make them look like new. He was wonderfully clever with his hands. He used to do embroidery and he made lovely kneelers for the local church. He also made little lead soldiers. He had these little moulds which he'd made himself and he made soldiers which he painted himself and displayed on the shelves in his shop. Occasionally he would give one to a special customer. He was quite a lot younger than me but he asked me to give up my work and move out to Isleworth where he had a nice little house with three bedrooms and a garden. He knew how I'd earned my living, of course, and he was never judgemental. But he didn't think it dignified for a woman of more mature years to have to work in that profession.'

'So I lived in Isleworth for quite a few years. It was very nice but a bit dull, to be honest. Lionel didn't enjoy good health. He smoked too much and suffered badly with his heart. His face and hands were more blue than pink and he used to get a lot of chest pains. He retired early and sold the shop and invested the money. He didn't have a pension but he put the money into the building society and we lived on a bit of interest for a while but we had to dig into the capital as well. Then when that ran out we sold the house in Isleworth and we moved out to a flat in Peckham. Lionel always knew that he'd go first and he told me that he'd put a bit of something aside for me so that I'd be all right. He said he'd put it in my trunk. I still had my trunk from when I'd been touring the music halls. I kept old stuff in it, rubbish mainly. I couldn't throw the trunk away. Not with being it so full of old memories. We aren't much more than the sum of our memories are we? Not really.'

'When he died, the flat had to be sold. I thought I'd be able to use what was left to pay rent but this couple turned up out of nowhere. I'd never known this because he hadn't mentioned it, but Lionel had been married and had a son. The son's wife saw something in the paper about Lionel having died and they came round and wanted whatever there was. Lionel and I were never married so they got everything. They said I could take Lionel's bits and pieces if I wanted them but that was only because they didn't want anything of his. I gave his clothes to a charity shop and most of the rest went out in the rubbish. All they wanted was the money. A nasty pair they were. He did something for the council and he thought he was very important. She was worse. She looked down her nose at me as though I were a bit of something she'd found stuck to the sole of her shoe.'

'Anyway,' said Miss Gwilliams, 'I packed up my stuff and the bits that Lionel had left and put it all in storage. He had a few bits of silver which they didn't know about and I sold those to keep me going for a while. Then I decided to come to Devon because I thought it would be cheaper and that the weather might be better. This cottage was the only place I could afford.'

That was her story.

Or, rather, it was her story up until the time she moved to Bilbury.

There was, however, something else.

A couple of weeks after she arrived in Bilbury, I visited and found her scrabbling on the floor of the room she used as a bed-sitting room. It was the sort of fussy room that Dr Brownlow would have described as crinkum-crankum. She was wheezing terribly as she did so for she had quite a nasty chest infection. A large metal bound trunk was open and she was surrounded by papers, boxes and all sorts of ephemera. Bobby, her much loved dog, was sitting on a chair looking down. 'If I'd made that mess, I'd be in all sorts of trouble,' he seemed to be saying.

Miss Gwilliams explained again that Lionel, the man with whom she had spent the last few years but to whom she had never been married, had assured her that he would ensure that she was looked after in her old age.

'He would never lie to me,' she said. 'And he must have suspected that his son would pop up out of the woodwork and take whatever money there was from the sale of the flat. He said he'd put something into my trunk and he made me promise not to look until I'd buried him.'

'What are those?' I asked, pointing to the gallimaufry of boxes, fal-lals, costumes and papers which were strewn across the floor.

'They were the things that were in my trunk,' said Miss Gwilliams. 'Some of it is my old rubbish. I'd forgotten about most of it. I haven't had this stuff out for years. But somewhere here there must be something valuable.'

I helped her look through the miscellaneous ephemera of her life. Old theatre bills and programmes were stuffed in an old brown envelope. One or two theatre posters bearing her name were rolled up and stored in a cardboard tube. There were some programmes from the Windmill Theatre and a few old perfume bottles; empty but still smelling faintly of the perfume they had contained, and, for Miss Gwilliams, no doubt reeking of memories. There were several brief and well-worn costumes, faded but neatly folded, and a number of items of lingerie which obviously bore memories.

She held one of the costumes up against her. It was boned like an old-fashioned corset, though smaller and more revealing, and covered with sequins.

'I used to wear this when I worked with the magician. When I was with him he called himself 'The Great Lugarno'. Magicians always called themselves 'The Great Something' in those days. Sidney, that was his real name, saw the name Lugarno in a travel agent's window. He didn't realise it was the name of a place. He just thought it was a good, foreign sounding name. My job was to distract the audience while he did something they weren't supposed to see. He used to make me lace my costume very tightly so that my bosom was bursting out of the top and looking as if it was about to escape. If he was having trouble with a trick, which happened very often I'm afraid, he used to whisper 'Bend'. I was then supposed to find some reason to bend forward so that the audience had a better view of my cleavage. I got into the habit of leaving little things on the stage – feathers usually – so that there was something for me to pick up when I'd bent forward. I was very flexible in those days so I could pick something off the stage without bending my knees.'

I picked up a tin box. It had once contained coffee. It was very heavy; so heavy, indeed, that I could hardly lift it. 'What on earth is in here?'

'Haven't the foggiest. It's not mine. It must be something that Lionel put in the trunk. Open it.'

I took off the lid. The tin was full of soldiers, all neatly painted. I carefully shook them out onto the floor. They looked to me as if they were soldiers from Napoleon's army at Waterloo. There were two types of soldier. One species was standing still and holding a rifle. The other type of soldier was marching. They were as heavy as lead soldiers always are.

'They're not worth anything are they?' There was hope in Miss Gwilliam's voice. But not much hope.

'Did Lionel make them?'

'Yes. Those are his. And look – this is in his handwriting.' She pulled a piece of paper out of the tin. It contained a few lines in a neat, compact writing. The handwriting of a craftsman. She showed it to me.

'To Gwladys: to keep you safe. My love, Lionel.'

That was all.

'To Gwladys: to keep you safe. My love, Lionel.'

It seemed an odd gift and an odd message.

'What are they worth?' she asked.

'I'm afraid they're probably not worth anything much. A few shillings.'

She picked up one of the soldiers, examined it and then threw it down; full of frustration and despair. A large flake of paint came off the soldier's back.

'Oh damn,' said Miss Gwilliams. 'Now look what I've done. Poor Lionel. He was so proud of his soldiers.'

I picked up the soldier, looking to see if it could be repaired. To my surprise, I saw that the soldier was not, after all, made of lead. Underneath the paint, the soldier was yellow not grey. But it was heavy: as heavy as lead or as heavy as...

'I think the soldier is made of gold,' I told her, holding up the damaged soldier for her to see.

She looked at me, then took the soldier from my hands.

'Gold? Really?'

'I'm sure it is,' I told her. 'They're heavy and yellow. At least this one is.'

'Knock the paint off another one!'

I hesitated. The soldiers were beautifully made.

'Go on!'

I took out my pocket knife and scratched a piece of paint from the second soldier. More yellow metal beneath the paint. I scratched the paint on a third soldier. Underneath the red and the blue there was yellow.

'I think they're all gold,' I told her. 'They're worth a small fortune.'

'Oh Lionel, you old darling!' said Miss Gwilliams. 'Bless your heart.' She started to cry.

Lionel had clearly poured gold into his moulds and made little gold soldiers. Then he had painted them to disguise what they were made of. I wondered why he'd felt the need to hide the gold. Maybe it was to deceive the relatives he knew might appear. Maybe it was to deceive someone else. Maybe Lionel was worried about death duties. Maybe the gold had not been acquired in an entirely legal manner. Lionel had, after all, worked in Soho and there have always been some rather dodgy people in that part of London.

'This is my legacy,' whispered Miss Gwilliams. 'He wasn't lying when he said he'd look after me.'

I took one of the soldiers to Patchy. He took it to a friend of his called Athol who deals in precious metals. Athol confirmed that the soldier was made of 22-carat gold.

We worked out that Miss Gwilliams could live comfortably for the rest of her life by just selling a soldier every now and then. And that's exactly what she decided to do. I think she enjoyed her final years in Bilbury.

She became quite delightfully feisty in her late 80s. On her 90th birthday party I remember her getting quite cross with a visitor who, having told her that she 'looked good for her age' said something patronising about it being 'nice to see older people still taking an interest in life'.

Miss Gwilliams, who did not like being talked down to as though she were a stupid child, told the visitor that she did not consider herself to be old.

'Oh!' said the visitor, clearly rather startled. 'So, what do you consider old?'

'Anyone who is at least ten years older than I am,' snapped Miss Gwilliams.

When she died of pneumonia, the indomitable Miss Gwilliams was 92-years-old and she had just four soldiers left in the old coffee tin. Bobby, her loyal, little dog, had died a year earlier.

In her will she left everything she had to the Bilbury Cottage Hospital though apart from the soldiers (which were very gratefully received and which enabled us to purchase several useful pieces of equipment including a hoist to help our not-so-young nursing staff and a ripple bed to help with nursing bedbound patients) there wasn't much to leave: just a trunk full of mementoes without the memories to keep them alive.

And after she had gone, River Cottage, the damp house by the river, was empty again.

The Lunchtime Robbers

It was lunchtime and we were sitting in the snug at the Duck and Puddle.

There were four of us: Patchy Fogg, who is our local antique dealer and whose visiting card describes him as a 'specialist in the sale of items of historical interest to discerning collectors from around the world', Frank Parsons, the genial landlord of the Duck and Puddle which, since it is the only hostelry in the village, he safely and accurately advertises as the oldest and the most welcoming inn in the village of Bilbury, Thumper Robinson, whose interests and professional activities could not possibly be listed on a visiting card small enough to fit into a pocket (and who would never consider having any cards printed even if they could), and myself.

There had been five of us but the fifth member of our company, Peter Marshall, the local village shopkeeper, had been called away on urgent business and had left us just a few moments earlier.

Peter would not tell us what it was that had necessitated him leaving the pub. It was, however, clearly something important for he had been looking at his watch every few minutes for the previous half an hour. And he had blushed a rather disconcerting shade of red when Patchy asked him where he was going. None of us had ever seen Peter blush before. I don't think any of us had even suspected that a retailer who advertises potatoes at five pence per pound, or 30 pence for five pounds, would know how to blush.

'It must be a woman,' said Thumper firmly.

'You mean Peter has an assignation?' said Patchy, sounding as astonished as I felt. Peter has been a bachelor ever since I first arrived in Bilbury and there has never been any hint that he might be interested in any human activity that did not involve the purchase, display and subsequent sale of a wide variety of popular comestibles.

Thumper shrugged, picked up the beer glass in front of him and drained what remained of his pint of Old Restoration.

'Crumbs,' said Frank. He frowned and then shook his head at Thumper's suggestion. Frank sometimes takes a little longer than other people to process new information. It is not unknown, for example, for Frank to laugh at a joke several minutes after everyone else has moved onto something else.

'Can't be possible,' said Patchy. 'He looked too miserable to have been planning an assignation.'

He was right. Peter had seemed preoccupied and rather depressed.

Patchy looked at his wrist, realised that he wasn't wearing a watch and then peered at the clock over the fireplace. 'Is that the right time?'

'It was half an hour fast when it stopped,' replied Frank with quiet certainty. He then thought for a moment. 'Or half an hour slow. I'm pretty sure it was one or the other. Gilly did tell me but I've forgotten. And there was a reason for it but I've forgotten what that was too.'

Patrons in a more conventional public house might have wondered how Frank could call 'Time' if he didn't know what the time was. This, however, was not something which concerned any of us since Frank usually called 'Time', and threw out any remaining customers, only when he was tired and decided he wanted to go to bed. I have known him close the bar at 2 a.m. and I have known him close it well before 8.00 p.m. in the evening.

Just then, the door burst open and three men tumbled into the snug.

One was carrying a pickaxe handle, one was carrying a cricket bat and one was carrying one of those cheap plastic guns which shoot dried peas. I recognised the gun because my flat mates and I all had similar weapons when I was a medical student.

The three men were all wearing balaclavas.

'This is a hold up!' shouted the one carrying the cricket bat.

We all looked at him and then at one another. We were all, I think, confused rather than alarmed. I could tell from their faces that my three companions were, like me, wondering why anyone would bother to raid the Duck and Puddle.

'Be careful with that thing,' I said to the man with the gun. 'If you fire it at someone's face you could blind them. A dried pea in the eye can be very nasty.'

117

He looked at me, then at the gun and then back at me. He scratched at the balaclava as though it were rather itchy which I suspect it was. It was cold outside but it was warm in the snug at the Duck and Puddle.

'Empty your pockets!' ordered the man with the cricket bat, who was either in charge or wanted to be in charge. He turned to Frank, who was sitting on a stool the other side of the bar. 'Are you the landlord?'

'It's my pub,' replied Frank.

'Open the till and give me everything you've got,' said the man with the cricket bat. 'But I don't want any small change. Just notes.'

'Haven't got any notes except a couple of old IOUs,' said Frank. He pressed the button which opened the till and then scooped out the contents which he laid out on the bar counter. 'Here you are,' he said. He counted it. 'There's 32p but I think one of the 10p coins is a bit dodgy to be honest. It looks to me as if it might have been made in someone's shed. I've been trying to get rid of it for weeks but we don't get a lot of people paying with real money so I don't get many opportunities to hand out change.'

'Is that all there is?' said the man with the cricket bat. He sounded terribly disappointed, as well he might have been. When you put on a balaclava, pick up a cricket bat and burst into a pub you don't expect to find yourself going home with just 32p more than you had when you set out.

'Afraid so.'

'What sort of pub is this?' demanded the robber.

'Not a very profitable one,' admitted Frank. 'Most of our customers put their drinks on the slate.' Frank reached below the counter and produced a small notebook which was his 1970s version of the old-fashioned slate upon which pub owners had traditionally kept score. He showed the robber the notebook and flicked through the pages. I felt rather guilty. My name was in there. But then so was Patchy's name and Thumper's name. The fact is that pretty well everyone in the village was in there. We tend to write out IOUs and leave them for Frank to write in his little notebook.

The man with the cricket bat raised his weapon above his shoulder, as though preparing for a drive through the covers, and turned away from Frank. 'You three!' he shouted. 'Empty your pockets.'

'Money, keys and fluff or just money?' demanded Thumper.

'Just money!'

Thumper reached into his pocket and a moment later spread a few coins on the table. 'There you are,' he said. 'Nine pence.'

'I can beat that,' said Patchy. He spread out the contents of his pockets. 'One penknife, a set of keys and 22p, much of it in copper I'm afraid.'

'I'm afraid I haven't got any cash with me,' I confessed. I don't usually bother carrying money unless I'm going outside Bilbury. I have a slate at the Duck and Puddle and run tabs with Peter Marshall at the village shop and with Reggie, at Tolstoy's, the local garage. There isn't anywhere else in the village where I need to buy anything. Actually, there isn't anywhere else where I could buy anything.

'This is bloody ridiculous!' said the man with the cricket bat, who seemed terribly upset.

'Take that bloody silly mask off, sit down and have a drink,' said Thumper. 'What would your Maureen say if she saw you poncing around looking like an extra in a cheap gangster movie.'

'What do you mean 'my Maureen'?'

'Your wife, you idiot,' said Thumper.

'How do you know who my wife is?'

'Because she works in the Post Office in Barnstaple. She's worked there for years. Everyone knows Maureen.'

'Oh.' He thought for a moment. 'How do you know she's my wife?'

'Because your name is 'Bone' Idol and you work at the timber yard in Bideford and you and I used to play football together when we were both younger and had nothing better to do than spend our Saturday afternoons running round in a muddy field.'

'Oh. How did you recognise me?'

'Well, a few things tipped me off,' said Thumper, who was clearly enjoying himself. 'First, you have a tattoo on your right hand which says 'Maureen', second you can't say your 'r's properly and third the timber yard van is parked outside.'

'I told you we shouldn't have come in the van!' said the man with the gun loaded with dried peas.

Frank scooped up the change from the bar counter and put it back into the till. Thumper and Patchy put their change back into their pockets. I would have put my change back into my pocket if I'd had any.

'Well how the hell else were we going to get here!' said the man with the cricket bat, whom I now knew to be Maureen's husband. It somehow changed things when I knew that he had a wife called Maureen who wouldn't approve of him robbing hostelries. 'We couldn't all climb on your bloody bicycle!'

'We could have come on the bus.'

'The buses only run on alternate Thursdays when there's a 'q' in the month,' snapped Maureen's husband.

The man with the plastic gun looked rather doleful at this.

'What months have got a 'q' in them?' asked the man with the pickaxe handle. Despite the balaclava mask he managed to look confused.

'Those balaclavas must be horribly itchy,' said Thumper.

'They're not balaclavas,' said the man with the pickaxe handle. 'They're ski masks. My Doreen knitted them from a pattern in her magazine.'

'Why don't we just tell them all our names?' demanded the man with the plastic gun.

'What do you mean?' demanded the man with the pickaxe handle.

'They already know who 'Bone' is, now they know your wife is called Doreen!'

'And your wife is called Thelma,' said Thumper. 'So just take the damned ski masks off,' he said. 'You all look like complete idiots. And if someone comes in they might get the wrong idea.'

The man with the cricket bat tore off his ski mask and stuffed it into his pocket. Underneath the mask he had a glum looking face. He was unfortunate in having exceptionally floppy ears. If you're planning a career as a hold-up man you don't want to have any instantly recognisable physical qualities but his ears were unique. If you were describing him to a policeman you would have just said, 'He had very floppy ears' and that would have been that. 'Oh yes,' the policeman would have said, 'we know who that is!' The glum looking man was red and clearly hot and appeared to be rather sticky. The other two took off their masks. They too looked red, hot and sticky.

'The one with the cricket bat is 'Bone' Idol,' said Thumper. 'The one with the pickaxe handle is Bill something and the one with the toy gun is Cedric Littlehampton. They all work at the timber yard.'

'Bill Blake,' said Bill something. 'My name is Bill Blake.'

'Can I try your pea gun?' I asked Cedric Littlehampton.

'Sure,' he replied, handing over his gun. 'You just aim and pull the trigger.'

'I remember,' I said. I aimed the gun at Frank and hit him in the chest with a dried pea.

'Oi!' said Frank, rubbing his chest. 'I manage to survive an armed raid and then I get shot by one of my customers!'

'Let me have a go!' said Patchy. I handed him the gun and he too shot Frank. Then Thumper had a go. He shot Frank twice and then shot me three times.

'This is brilliant!' said Patchy. 'We could organise an indoor shooting competition. We could get four of these and have a battle.'

'I hope someone is going to pick up all these bullets,' said Frank.

'They're dried peas,' I reminded him. 'If you collect enough of them you could make a soup or put them in a stew.'

'Gilly makes a lovely soup with dried peas,' said Frank, who was justifiably proud of his wife's cooking. 'She just puts the peas into a pan, pours in some water, adds a few carrots and half a dozen bay leaves and then throws in a handful of her croutons when she serves it. It's one of our most popular soups during the winter months.'

'One of my favourites,' agreed Patchy with a nod of approval.

'Pretty good,' agreed Thumper. 'But I prefer the cock-a-leekie. Gilly makes the best cock-a-leekie I've ever tasted.'

'Please don't use all my ammunition,' begged Cedric. He crawled around, picking up all the peas he could find. 'I borrowed the gun and the ammunition from my boy Jason and he counted the peas before he handed them over.'

'You won't tell anyone about this, will you?' begged the man called 'Bone'.

'You haven't done anything to tell anyone about,' said Thumper, with a shrug.

'They came into the pub waving weapons!' Frank pointed out with unarguable accuracy. 'It was an armed robbery.'

'For God's sake don't tell Maureen,' pleaded 'Bone', the ring-leader, who was still holding his cricket bat. 'If you're going to tell

Maureen I'd rather you called the cops. I'd rather do ten years in the nick than explain this cock-up to our Maureen.'

'I didn't know your timber yard had started making pickaxe handles,' said Thumper.

'Oh yes, we've been making them for a few months. How did you know we make them?'

'The handle is stamped with the company logo,' explained Thumper.

The man examined the handle. 'Oh,' he said. 'So it is.'

'So is one of you going to buy us all a drink?' asked Patchy.

The three intruders all looked at him.

'You've come all the way from Barnstaple,' said Patchy. 'You must be thirsty. And if you're going to have a round of drinks you ought to include us. It would be rude not to.'

'I'll have another pint, please,' said Thumper. 'Old Restoration.'

'Glass of Chablis, if you don't mind,' said Patchy. 'Better make it a large one. I've just had a terrifying experience. I'm suffering from that thing…' he turned to me. 'What is it?'

'Shell shock,' I said. 'I'll have a Laphroaig.'

'I'll just take a large gin,' said Frank.

'No you won't,' said Gilly, who had appeared from nowhere and who is looking after Frank's health with great attentiveness to detail. 'You'll have a nice tonic water with a big, thick, juicy slice of lemon in it.'

'These gentleman are paying,' muttered Frank. 'They're buying a round of drinks. With real money.'

'Then you can charge them for a large gin but give yourself a tonic water,' said Gilly. 'I'll have a port and lemon.'

'Yes, dear,' said Frank glumly.

'I'll have a beer,' said the man with the plastic gun.

'Me too,' said 'Bone', the man with the cricket bat. 'Give the man some money,' he said to Bill, the man with the pickaxe handle.

'Why me?' demanded Bill.

'We'll settle up with you later.'

'No, you won't,' said Bill. 'You always say you will but you never do. I paid for the petrol we put in the van and you said you'd settle up with me later. I paid for the wool for these bloody silly balaclavas. I'm always the one who gets lumbered with the bill.'

'They're ski masks.'

'No, they're not. They're bloody balaclavas. And it's not fair!'

'Well, I haven't got any money with me.'

Bill, the man with the pickaxe handle took out a wallet, removed a £5 note and put it down on the counter. 'Give me a receipt with my change,' he said wearily. 'And I'll have half a shandy.'

Frank poured the drinks and put a few coins and a till receipt on the counter. He then reached down into a box on the floor by his feet and, one by one, counted out twenty seven packets of crisps and eleven packets of pork scratchings. He then added two boxes of matches to the pile.

'What are these for?' asked Bill, staring at the packets of crisps and pork scratchings and the boxes of matches.

'I haven't got any more change,' explained Frank. 'You'll have to take those in lieu of what I owe you. Or I can put you down in the book as having a credit of two pounds and thirty seven pence.'

'I'll take the crisps and stuff,' sighed the unhappy robber. He leant the pickaxe handle against the wall, picked up the snacks and started stuffing them into his jacket pockets. When his pockets were full, he looked at Frank and waved a hand over the remaining pile of crisps and pork scratchings. 'Do you have anything I can put these in?'

Frank reached down, lifted up the empty cardboard box from which he had taken the crisps and put it down on the bar. 'You can have this for free,' he said. 'Compliments of the management.'

'Thanks,' said Bill. He didn't sound terribly grateful.

'Can I have a packet of those?' asked Cedric, the ersatz gunman. 'Salt and vinegar preferably. I'm a bit peckish, but the cheese and onion ones always give me wind.'

'No, you can't!' snapped Bill, who was clearly not happy. 'Buy your own bloody crisps.' He transferred the crisps, the pork scratchings and the matches from the bar counter to the box and then added the packets he had already stuffed into his pockets.

'I hope you don't mind my mentioning it but I think you need a better plan if you're going to do this again,' said Thumper. 'And maybe you need to go somewhere you aren't likely to be recognised.'

'I'm not doing this again,' said the man with the pickaxe handle and the box of assorted snacks. 'I can't afford to be a robber.'

'Nice beer,' said the man with his boy's toy gun. He spotted another dried pea on the floor, bent down, picked it up, brushed off a bit of fluff and put it into his pocket with the rest of his ammunition.

'Does anyone want a sandwich?' asked Gilly. 'We've got ham or cheese.'

'No thanks, love,' said the man with the cricket bat. He looked at his watch. 'We came over in our lunchtime. We'd better be getting back.'

'The Lunchtime Robbers!' said Thumper, writing an imaginary headline in the air.

The man with the cricket bat growled and muttered something.

The three robbers drank up, said goodbye and left.

'They seem like nice fellows,' said Patchy, when they'd gone.

'But perhaps not too bright,' said Thumper.

'No, perhaps not too bright.'

'I've got a £5 note in the till!' said Frank excitedly. He took the note out and examined it carefully as though it were the first time he'd ever seen a £5 note. Come to think of it, it may well have been the first £5 note he had seen for quite a while.

'I'd better take that and put it somewhere safe,' said Gilly, taking the note from between his fingers.

'And I'd better get back to my showroom,' said Patchy. 'I've got a customer coming to look at another bed that King Charles II slept in. It's the last bed he slept in before he climbed up into that famous oak tree.'

'How do you know Charles II slept in it?' asked Frank, who can sometimes show flashes of surprising naivety and still doesn't entirely understand the extent of the grey area in which Patchy operates. 'How can you really prove it? Did he carve his initials on a bedpost?'

Patchy, who has to my knowledge sold eight of the beds in which King Charles II is alleged to have slept, looked at Frank slightly disbelievingly and then turned to Gilly. 'Is that clock over the fireplace 30 minutes fast or 30 minutes slow?'

Frank, abandoning hope of an answer to his question, picked up a tray and started to collect the empty glasses left by our trio of armed robbers.

Gilly frowned, thought for a moment and then shrugged. 'I can't remember,' she said. 'No one has ever asked me that before. But I'm

124

pretty sure you're right: it was either 30 minutes fast or 30 minutes slow when it stopped, if that's any help.'

'That's OK,' said Patchy, with a sigh. He looked out of the window. 'It's light out so it must still be afternoon.'

And with that he wandered off to sell another bed which had been slept in by King Charles II. If Patchy could have found a decent ringer for the Boscobel oak tree which the King climbed in order to escape Oliver Cromwell's Roundhead soldiers, he would have happily sold that too. Patchy has an antique dealer's approach to historical truth; it is one based more on hope than fact, more on belief and expectation than vanilla flavoured verisimilitude.

'Where's Peter?' asked Gilly. 'I thought I heard him here earlier.'

'I think he had an assignation,' said Thumper. 'He hurried off a while ago.'

'Ah,' said Gilly. 'That'll be an assignation with his fiancée. I think she wanted to see him to discuss the wedding. Her mother is staying with her to help with the planning. She came down on the train yesterday. Jake, who brought her over in his taxi, says she's apparently a pleasant enough woman, if you like overbearing, domineering women with lots of blue hair.'

'What!' exclaimed Thumper and I simultaneously.

'What did you say?' demanded Frank.

'Pleasant woman, if you like overbearing, domineering women with lots of blue hair,' repeated Gilly. She paused for a moment, clearly thinking. 'She looks a bit like one of those carved figureheads you see fixed to the front of sailing ships; acres of hair and a solid-looking, rather menacing bosom.'

'No, no, not that bit,' said Frank. 'The bit about Peter having a fiancée.'

'Didn't you know?' asked Gilly. 'Hasn't he told you? He and Hilda Musbury are getting married. He hired her to run the estate agency for him and they seem to have hit it off together.' She smiled. 'Or maybe she just made him an offer he couldn't refuse.'

Thumper, Frank and I stared at her.

We were speechless, so we said nothing.

It occurred to me that, when he had left us, Peter hadn't looked like a happy bridegroom off to meet his beloved. He'd looked more like a man with a fixed date with an executioner.

I was pretty sure that the same thought had occurred to Thumper and to Frank.

Peter's Great Escape

Within less than 24 hours of my hearing that Peter Marshall and Hilda Musbury were engaged to be married, Patsy and I received a letter, addressed to us both, which contained a list of 'acceptable wedding presents' for the happy couple. The letter was signed by Hilda but not by Peter.

Patsy opened the letter and passed it to me without saying a word.

I looked down the list. Every item on the list had the price beside it. To my astonishment there wasn't anything on it which cost less than £10!

That was a good deal of money for us and for most people living in Bilbury.

Back in the early 1970s, you could buy a gallon of petrol for 33p, a pound of potatoes for 5p, a ticket for the Cup Final for £2 and a long-playing record for £3.

You could buy a Mini Cooper, an excellent and powerful new car for £600. And even in expensive parts of the country, a very decent family house wouldn't set you back much more than £5,000. In Bilbury, you could buy a cottage for £3,000. And Tolstoy's, our local garage, had a variety of cars for sale for between £30 and £100. It is true that they all had a few dings and there was a bit of rust here and there on the bodywork, but they all ran reasonably well and the four tyres, while perhaps not in the first flush of youth, still had a few miles left in them. Reggie always put a bit of black paint over very bald bits of tyre where the canvas was showing through.

(Reggie, who runs the garage, has never believed in providing a spare wheel. He says that not having a spare wheel means that there is more luggage space in the boot.)

Apart from the expense, the other odd thing about the list was that everything on it seemed to have been chosen by Hilda.

I really couldn't see Peter making out a list which included: ice cream maker, home perm kit, sandwich maker, waffle maker, food mixer, coffee machine, hot plate, hostess trolley, home bust

127

enlarging course (audio tape and book), electric wok, Chinese rug (dimensions supplied), Cartier tank watch (ladies), telephone answering machine, chair covers (measurements supplied), Polaroid camera, electric hair curlers, pearl necklace with matching earrings, two way stretch girdle in white or mocha (size supplied on request), combination alarm clock and tea maker, matching luggage from Louis Vuitton and a vanity case in alligator hide.

'Do you think Peter knows what is on this list?' asked Patsy.

I said I didn't think Peter had even seen the letter let alone the list that accompanied it.

Now, it is perfectly true that Peter has been justifiably described as greedy and as a bit of a skinflint. And there is no doubt that he is always on the lookout for ways to gouge another penny or two from his customers.

For example, just the other day I bought a pack of three green peppers from him and it was only when he told me the price that I realised that he was charging more for the package of peppers than he would have charged if I had bought three loose peppers.

'But I had to put the three peppers into a pack,' Peter explained indignantly. 'So it is entirely reasonable to charge more for the convenience.'

I put the pack back on the shelf, picked out three peppers and bought those for 5p less.

Peter then told me that he was charging 5p for every brown paper bag a customer took. I stuffed the peppers into my pockets and stuck my tongue out at him.

I confess I rather enjoy these silly little battles with Peter. You can't have that sort of fun when shopping in a supermarket.

But knowing all this meant that I couldn't help thinking that Peter knew the value of money far too well to expect his friends and customers to put their hands quite so deeply into their pockets.

We were still talking about the wedding list, and wondering what on earth we should do about it, when the telephone went. It was Adrienne, Patsy's sister and Patchy Fogg's wife. She was so cross that I could hear her side of the conversation as well as Patsy's.

'Have you had one of these wedding lists from Peter Marshall?' Adrienne demanded, shouting so much that we didn't really need the telephone to hear her. She and Patchy only live a couple of miles away and if we'd opened a window we would have heard her without it.

'I think it came from Hilda rather than Peter,' said Patsy.

'Is she mad?' asked Adrienne who is renowned for having a short fuse and speaking her mind. 'Have you seen the prices of some of the things on her list? When Patchy and I got married, Peter gave us a 5lb sack of potatoes as a wedding present!'

Patsy said that at least the potatoes were useful and pointed out that when we got married Peter had given us a large box of fly papers. The fly papers were those sticky streamers that you hang from the ceiling but they were so old that they had lost their stickiness and were entirely useless.

'Who does she think is going to buy her a Cartier tank watch?' demanded Adrienne, who sounded as if she had steam coming out of both ears.

'Do you know how many people have had one of these letters?' asked Patsy.

'Mum and Dad got one,' said Adrienne. They get their post earlier than we do and Mum was on the telephone twenty minutes ago.'

'I feel sorry for Peter,' said Patsy.

'And what does Hilda want with a bust enlarging and firming course?' demanded Adrienne. 'I would have hardly thought she would have needed assistance in that department!'

'Maybe it's for Peter,' suggested Patsy.

There was loud laughter and some snorting from the other end of the telephone.

At this point, I decided that I would pop into the consulting room and start the morning's work. I kissed Patsy, made my silent excuses and left.

But if I thought I had heard the last of the wedding list saga, I was making a huge mistake.

Peter turned up at my evening surgery that day. I couldn't remember the last time I'd seen him professionally.

'I need help,' he said, before he'd even sat down.

'O.K. Tell me what help you need and how I can help.'

'I suppose you've seen that letter that Hilda sent out?' he said, moving the patient's chair around before sitting down.

'The one with the list of recommended wedding presents?'

'That's the one,' said Peter. He sighed wearily. 'That list is making my life miserable.' He paused and blew his nose. 'Your friend Thumper Robinson wanted to know if a bag of gold sovereigns would be satisfactory as a present – even though they're not on the list.'

'There's bound to be some teasing,' I said. 'You're getting married for the first time.'

'I can't bear the thought of being married to that damned woman,' said Peter suddenly.

'Ah,' I said. 'All things considered I can see that could be a bit of a problem.'

'I've started wondering whether I should kill her or kill myself.'

'Hmm,' was the best I could manage in response to this gloomiest of gloomy thoughts.

'At first I thought she'd make a great estate agent,' said Peter. 'You recommended her to me.' He paused and thought for a while. 'So really it's your fault that I'm in this mess!'

'Oh, wait a minute, Peter,' I said, rather defensively. 'You were looking for someone to run your new estate agency. I suggested Hilda and you thought she'd be right for the job. I didn't recommend that you married her!'

'She hasn't sold a single house since she started work,' said Peter miserably. 'Not one! She annoys the sellers by telling them why she doesn't like their taste in furniture and decorations and puts off the buyers by telling them what's wrong with every house they look at.'

'How did you come to ask her to marry you?' I asked him.

'I didn't ask her to marry me!' said Peter, indignantly.

'So what happened?'

'I suppose she sort of asked me.'

'She asked you to marry her?'

'Well, she didn't so much ask me as tell me we were getting married.'

'She told you to marry her?' I said, incredulously.

'She said it would be best if we married.'

'Best? Best for whom? Best for what?'

'That's what I wondered. But that's what we she said.'

'Hang on a minute, Peter,' I said. 'Can we go back a step or two? You hired her to run your new estate agency. What happened between that and her telling you that it would be best if you got married? There must have been something in between.'

'We seemed to be getting on well,' said Peter, closing his eyes as he remembered. 'One day we were having lunch together, just a tin of oxtail soup and some out-of-date crackers that needed eating up, and I said I would like to see more of her.'

Peter then moved his chair around a little before returning it to its original position. I waited. I had known him since shortly after I had arrived in Bilbury but I had never before seen him so utterly beaten.

'I said I'd like to see a little more of her,' he said. 'I thought we could go to Ilfracombe and watch the fishermen. Or take a walk down to Heddon's Mouth.'

'That sounds fine to me. What happened then?'

'She got all coy and looked at me as though she was a bit shocked and then she giggled a lot and unfastened the top two buttons of her blouse and said: 'How much more of me would you like to see, Peter?' Peter gulped, clearly still horrified at what had happened. 'When I said I wanted to see more of her I was speaking in general terms. But she, er, interpreted my remark in a very literal sort of way.'

'Oh. Oh dear. I see.'

'She kept unfastening buttons and then she pulled the two sides of her blouse apart and asked me if this was what I wanted to see.' Peter paused. 'She was wearing a bra but she's a big woman, doctor, and there was a lot of, well, bosom, flowing over the top of it.'

I made an encouraging noise to keep him going.

'I didn't know what to say or where to look,' said Peter, who was now blushing. 'So I put down my soup and held out both hands to try to cover her up a bit and to stop her unfastening anything else.'

I thought I could see what probably happened next.

'She thought I was trying to touch her and she grabbed my hands and sort of put them onto her, you know...'

'Breasts?'

'Yes. Those.'

'Then what happened?' I asked.

'Nothing! Absolutely nothing. I managed to get free and I rushed off to unpack a case of cat food that had come in that morning.'

'Did she come after you?'

131

'She wouldn't leave me alone! She kept rubbing up against me and breathing funny and saying my name a lot and whenever we were alone together she would try to put my hands onto her chest.'

'So when did she suggest that the two of you got married?'

'A couple of days after the unbuttoning thing happened. She was helping me lay out some parsnips and radishes when she suddenly said she thought it would be best, all things considered, if we got married.'

'And what did you say?'

'I don't think I said anything. I was horrified! I didn't want to marry the woman then and I even more don't want to marry her now – not after that letter and all those things she put on the damned silly list.'

'Have you said anything to her? Have you told her that you don't want to get married?'

'I've tried!' said Peter. 'Heaven knows I've tried. But she takes no notice. She just tells me I've got the usual bridegroom nerves and asks me where I want to go for the honeymoon. As if I can go off on a honeymoon? Who will look after the shop if I go off on a honeymoon? I told her she'd have to go on her own.'

'You told her she'd have to go on the honeymoon by herself?'

'Yes. Yes. I did.'

He shuffled on the chair and looked embarrassed, as if telling the truth was a slightly shameful exercise. Maybe he also thought the truth was scarcely believable and felt bad because it was all he had to offer.

'What did she say to that?'

'She said I didn't mean that and that we'd have a wonderful time and she sort of winked at me and said it probably didn't really matter where we went because we wouldn't be going out much anyway because I'd probably be wanting to have my wicked way with her all the time.'

'That's what she said: 'you'd be wanting to have your wicked way with her'?'

'Yes,' said Peter glumly. 'Exactly that.'

Peter had never struck me as the sort of person likely to want to have his wicked way with anyone. He was the more the sort of fellow who regarded a 'good time' as synonymous with 'a healthy profit'.

'And now she's moved into my flat above the shop and her mother has come to stay,' said Peter who has lived in a small flat above the village shop for as long as he or I can remember.

'Hilda is living with you?'

'She announced that she was moving into my place so that we could save money,' said Peter. 'She said it was silly for her to pay rent on a cottage when I had a spare room.'

'So you haven't, er, been sleeping together?'

Peter stared at me as if I'd gone mad. 'No! No! Certainly not.'

'Of course not,' I agreed. 'And why did her mother come to stay with you?'

'Hilda said that since she was living in my flat and we weren't married she needed her mother to stay as a chaperone.'

'Ah.'

'Exactly. And her mother is just like Hilda only more so. She's called Hilda too.'

'When is the wedding fixed for?'

'I've no idea,' said Peter. 'She went off this morning to fix a date with the vicar. Her mother went with her.' Peter swallowed and looked at me. The look reminded me of the look I get from Ben the dog when I'm eating something he wants to share. 'Together, they're an unstoppable force.'

I pitied Peter. The idea of living with two Hildas was not something I could contemplate without trepidation. The world was not a big enough place for two Hildas.

'Have you told Hilda that you don't, er, want to get married?' I asked him.

Peter looked at me as if I were out of my mind.

'You can't tell Hilda anything,' said Peter glumly. 'She never listens.'

'You're going to have to find a way to make her understand,' I told him.

'Can't you help?' asked Peter. He sounded rather pathetic – like a small boy who is being bullied at school and wants his Dad to sort things out.

'I'll try to think of something,' I told him. 'But I don't think you should pin your hopes on me.'

'Thanks!' said Peter, with a smile. 'That's great.'

It was clear that he'd heard my first sentence but had completely ignored the second. He stood up, nodded and left, looking much brighter than he'd looked when he'd arrived.

I spent much of the day thinking about Peter's problem and getting absolutely nowhere. I really couldn't think of a way out – other than encouraging Peter to find the courage to sit Hilda down and explain to her that he didn't want to get married, had never asked her to marry him and had absolutely no intention of marrying her.

That seemed a remote possibility.

Poor old Peter.

And then, to my astonishment, Hilda Musbury turned up at my evening surgery.

'I'm getting married,' she told me, as if this were news to me. 'And naturally I'm going to need some sort of contraceptive advice.' She smiled sweetly. 'I told Pete that I'd pop along and talk to you about contraceptives. I don't think we want to be using those rubbery things.'

Although she is a widow, Mrs Musbury somehow managed to sound as if she were a virginal bride who had no idea what thrills and spills might await her in the marital bed. Nevertheless, Hilda did not appear to me to be a nervous maiden; waiting for the moment when she would blossom into womanhood; anticipating a ceremonial deflowering with great anxiety.

Actually, considering Peter's lack of enthusiasm, it seemed to me that there were unlikely to be any large waves crashing onto her rocky shoreline and nor were there likely to be any steam trains vanishing into long, dark, smoky tunnels.

I didn't think Peter would much like being called 'Pete' either. I've never known anyone call him 'Pete'.

'How old are you, Mrs Musbury?' I asked her, pretending to look through her medical notes for the information I already had.

'Forty two,' she said immediately.

I looked at her and waited.

'Forty nine?' she tried, half pleading, half wheedling.

'Have another attempt.'

'Fifty five,' she said flatly, cross to have been found out, though she should have known I would have the correct figure somewhere in her medical notes.

'And you went through the menopause four years ago I think? I seem to remember there was…' I flicked through her medical records.

'Oh that, yes,' she said flatly.

'That's good!' I said. 'In that case I don't think you'll be needing any contraceptive advice. You can just…er…well enjoy each other au naturel.'

'Oh, that's a nice surprise!' said Hilda, as though delighted by this revelation. 'I'm sure Pete will be thrilled. I know what men are like about these things.' She tried to wink but failed miserably. The failure made her look gauche and sly at the same time.

'Are you going on a honeymoon?' I asked her.

I'd suddenly had the germ of an idea.

'I haven't been able to tie him down yet,' she said. 'He cares so much about his shop.' She said this as though she were in competition with the shop for his affection though she probably did not realise that in truth she was and had already lost the contest. 'He says he can't take time away from it. But everyone knows that little shop must be a goldmine. I want us to go to a smart hotel somewhere. Venice, Rome or Paris perhaps. We'll perhaps take mother along for a treat.' She smirked. It was a very unpleasant smirk. 'He can afford it.'

'Really?' I said.

'Oh yes. Pete's a very wealthy man.'

'Who told you that?' I asked. I knew Peter wouldn't have said anything of the sort.

'Everyone knows he's wealthy. Don't they?' She began to look just a little bit concerned.

'Gosh! I don't think so. Have you thought that he may be reluctant to fix a honeymoon because he can't afford to take time away from the shop,' I said. 'And maybe he can't afford an expensive honeymoon. He did say something about a possible three day camping holiday in Cornwall. Patchy has a small tent which I'm sure he'd be happy to lend the pair of you.'

Hilda paled and looked shocked.

'A tent?'

'Quite roomy for two,' I said. 'And pretty well waterproof unless the weather is really bad.'

'Oh.'

'And I think he did mention to me that he wondered if it would be all right if he asked your mother for a loan.' I said. I then hesitated. 'You mustn't mention any of this to anyone,' I said.

She promised she wouldn't.

I had my fingers crossed under the desk. I didn't feel bad about the fib. This marriage was clearly going to be a disaster for both parties. It would be as much of a disaster for Hilda as for Peter.

'My mother? He wanted a loan from my mother?'

'Just £500 or so to tide him over. He's going through a bit of a bad patch, I think. I heard one of the wholesalers was chasing him over some long overdue unpaid bills. I don't think they've threatened to send the bailiffs in yet but I suppose it's only a matter of time.'

'Unpaid bills?' said Hilda. She had gone very pale.

Since I had been the one to bring the two of them together I felt I owed Peter this bit of help.

'Still, having a loving wife will be good for him,' I said. 'You can share the burdens. A trouble shared is a trouble halved, don't they say? If your mother can come up with a loan then I'm sure everything will be fine. And if things do go bad I'm sure you'll both be happy living in a caravan – or even in Patchy's little tent. True love conquers all, doesn't it?'

Hilda got up, said goodbye and sped from the room as though she'd suddenly realised she'd left the gas on at home.

An hour after I'd finished the surgery, I was sitting with a cup of coffee and a small glass of malt whisky when the door-bell rang.

It was Peter. He was holding a paper bag and a small parcel wrapped in brown paper. The parcel was tied with string and a little loop had been created so that the holder of the parcel could carry it on one finger. He thrust the bag and the parcel at me before he'd crossed the threshold.

I opened the paper bag. It contained four pears. I untied the string on the small parcel. Inside the parcel there were two small bottles of shampoo.

'What are these for?'

'A thank you! A big thank you. Hilda came to see you this evening didn't she?'

'She did.'

'What did you say to her?'

136

'Oh you know, just a bit of this and a bit of that. We had a chat about you and weddings and honeymoons and contraceptives.'

'She's broken it off!'

'The wedding?'

'Of course, the wedding. She said she'd had a chat with you and she realised that maybe we aren't quite right for each other. She and her mother packed and were out of the house within an hour.' He suddenly stopped. 'Contraceptives? Why did you talk about contraceptives?'

'Can't talk about these things,' I told him. 'Secrets of the consulting room.'

'What did you tell her?' demanded Peter.

I grinned at him. 'Nothing for you to worry about, I promise. But don't do anything flashy to celebrate your escape,' I told him. 'Just remember, you're broke and want to borrow £500 from her mother.'

Peter is many things but he isn't slow.

'Thank you,' he said. He nodded at the bag of pears I was holding. 'They're ready to eat straight away,' he said. I looked into the bag. The pears were certainly on the downward slope side of ripeness. 'And the shampoo is excellent stuff. Patsy will love it.' I looked at the bottles of shampoo. The word 'Sample' was printed on each bottle. I thanked him.

As he started to leave I called out.

'Peter!'

He turned round.

I grinned at him. 'What are you doing about the estate agency?'

'I'm closing it,' he said brusquely. 'Shut and gone for ever.'

And he shuddered visibly as he walked to his van.

I took the overripe pears and the shampoo samples in and showed them to Patsy.

'Where on earth did you get those?'

'Peter brought them. As a gift.'

'It's not your birthday, is it?'

I laughed. Peter is not renowned for his generosity.

'These pears are very soft.'

'Cedric will like them.'

And indeed Cedric the pig munched his way through them in no time at all.

We're planning to give Peter the shampoo as a Christmas present. I hope he recognises it and welcomes it back home.

The Reluctant Jumper

Ephraim Hardstaff is a cautious, careful, meticulous man.

It is said that when he was a lad he was the only boy in the village who would walk round puddles so that his shoes never got wet or muddy. He would, it is said, do this even if he was wearing Wellington boots.

He is the sort of person who always does crossword puzzles in pencil and will only fill in an answer in ink when he is absolutely certain that he's got the right solution.

But Ephraim is also a good hearted, kindly and gentle man.

He is the sort of fellow who moves snails off a path or roadway so that they don't get accidentally trodden on or run over. He rescues injured birds and once nursed a young deer back to health after it had been hit by a delivery lorry. Whenever a good cause needs a volunteer or a donation he is at the front of the queue: always ready to give whatever he can to help other people. There is no doubt that if the world contained more Ephraim Hardstaffs it would be a better, warmer place.

He was sitting on the other side of my consulting room desk. And he looked worried.

'I can't sleep,' said Ephraim. 'Could you give me something to help me?'

'How long has this been going on?' I asked.

'About three months.'

'Is it getting better or worse or just the same?'

'It's getting worse. I used to get off to sleep eventually but now it takes me hours to drop off. And then I wake up again after about half an hour.'

'Do you have any pain?' I asked. Surprisingly, perhaps, pain is one of the most important causes of insomnia.

'No, no, no pain,' said Ephraim.

'How well did you sleep up until three months ago?'

'No problem. Never any problem at all.'

'So what's happened to change things? What's different in your life? Is there anything different about your bedroom? New bed?'

'No, no,' said Ephraim. 'Same old bed, same old bedroom.'

'Is Daphne sleeping all right?' I asked him. Daphne is his wife. She too is a sweet, kind, gentle individual.

'Not very well,' said Ephraim. 'I think she's probably going to come and see you about it.'

'So both of you are having trouble sleeping?'

'Yes, that's right.'

'What is it?'

'What's what?' he asked.

'Something is worrying you both, something is keeping you awake. I can't help you unless you tell me what it is.'

'Can't you just give me some sleeping tablets?'

I shook my head. 'Not until I know why you're not sleeping.'

There was a pause for a moment. 'I've signed up for something,' said Ephraim suddenly. 'When I said I'd do it I just said 'yes' without really thinking about it. And at the time the whole thing seemed a long way away. But now it's getting closer and I'm worrying a lot about it.'

'And Daphne is worrying about it too?'

'Yes. She is.'

'So what did you sign up for?'

'A parachute jump.'

'You signed up for a parachute jump?'

'Yes.'

Internally I sighed.

I am always amazed at the way so many people misunderstand risk. Indeed, the world seems to be full of people who have no real concept of what is risky and what is not as risky. People worry about all the wrong things and often fail to understand just how significant some risks can be. People assume that boxing is a dangerous sport but in fact it is probably safer than riding a horse or playing rugby. The risks associated with eating the wrong sort of foods are actually far greater than the risks involved in drinking a modest amount of alcohol. The risk to your health of being overweight is far greater than most other risks and yet it is a risk many still tend to ignore. Health and safety rules often fail to take into account the significance of some risks when compared with others.

And parachuting out of an aeroplane is an enormously risky activity – especially for individuals who are inexperienced and who are neither trained for it nor particularly fit.

A few hours of on the spot training, really doesn't make much difference. The number of people who jump out of aeroplanes in the hope of raising money for charity, but who end up in hospital is frighteningly high.

'When?'

'In a month's time. A charity in South Molton organised it. They're raising money to help children in India.'

'And how will you jumping out of an aeroplane help children in India?'

'I'm supposed to find sponsors. People who will give money if I jump out of an aeroplane.'

I'd heard of this bizarre way of raising money for charity. It had become very fashionable. Quite a lot of charities were encouraging their supporters to raise money by jumping out of aeroplanes.

'Have you got any sponsors?'

'Not yet,' admitted Ephraim.

'Have you tried?'

'Not really. Well, no, to be honest, not at all.'

'Why not?'

'Because I was worried that I might panic and not want to jump out of the aeroplane and then I wouldn't raise any of the money I'd said I'd raise. And it would be very embarrassing too.'

'And it's because you've been worrying about the parachute jump that you haven't been able to sleep?'

'Yes,' admitted Ephraim. 'And it's been keeping Daphne awake too. She's worried that I'll break a leg or an arm or even my back.'

'So why don't you just tell them that you've changed your mind?'

'Oh, I couldn't do that,' said Ephraim. 'I'd feel that I was letting them down.'

'But you don't have to jump out of an aeroplane to raise money for them? Do something else? Stand in Barnstaple High Street with a collecting tin. Sell pictures of the children they're saving. There must be a hundred ways you can help them without risking life and limb by jumping out of an aeroplane. '

'The person who is organising it all is someone I work with,' said Ephraim. 'They already think I'm a bit of a wimp. If I tell them I'm backing out they'll tell everyone I was chicken.'

'And that worries you?'

'Yes. I know it shouldn't do but it does. I'm a bit sensitive like that.'

'Are you still working at that shoe shop in Barnstaple?' I asked him.

'Yes.'

'And that's where the organiser of the jump works?'

'Yes. Dicky is the organiser. There are six of us working in the shop and Dicky is one of the other five.'

'Dicky is the organiser of the jump?'

'Yes. I don't think he cares much about the children to be honest. But he wanted to jump out of an aeroplane without having to pay for it. So he signed up to jump and then said he'd recruit some more people to do it.'

'And you said 'yes' because you always say 'yes', because you didn't want to disappoint him and because the day of the jump seemed so far away that you weren't worried about it because you thought the day might never arrive?'

Ephraim smiled. 'That's about it, yes.'

I had an idea.

'Will you be working next Wednesday?'

'Oh yes. I work every day.'

'And Dicky will be there?'

'Yes.'

'OK. Here's what's going to happen. I'm going to come in to your shop to buy some shoelaces. When you see me, you come over, you tell me about the jump and ask me if I'll sponsor you.'

'How will that help?' he asked.

'Trust me,' I said.

I was due to go into Barnstaple the following Wednesday so when I'd finished my business at the bank I went into the shoe shop where Ephraim worked.

As soon as I had bought my shoelaces Ephraim, as arranged, came over to me, showed me some sponsorship forms and asked if I would sponsor him to jump out of an aeroplane.

'I most certainly will not!' I said, raising my voice so that everyone in the shop could hear. 'Are you mad? There was a paper in the *British Medical Journal* the other week proving that the cost of treating all the people who jump out of aeroplanes and injure themselves far outweighs the money that is raised by people jumping out of aeroplanes. I know of people who are paraplegics, permanently paralysed, because they jumped out of aeroplanes. Hundreds of people have broken hips or shattered their spines. You must be mad. And you must think I'm mad if you think I'm going to encourage such stupid behaviour.'

'But...' began Ephraim, who seemed a little startled by my outburst.

I took the forms from him, ripped them up and put them down onto the counter. 'I suggest you put these into the bin,' I told him. 'If you go ahead with this daft jump I'll have you certified insane.'

'Oh. All right, doctor,' said Ephraim, who still looked surprised. 'If you really think so.'

'I know so!' I said loudly. 'The people who do this are ignorant idiots. And the people who organise these damned parachute jumps are ignorant idiots too.'

I couldn't help noticing that one of Ephraim's colleagues had gone bright red.

I then stalked out of the shop clutching my new shoelaces.

As I left, I heard one of the assistants say to Ephraim. 'Who on earth was that?'

'My doctor,' said Ephraim.

'Golly,' said the assistant. 'He's a bit frightening isn't he? I'm glad he's not my doctor.' From what I could gather as I left, this viewpoint seemed to be greeted with some approval.

Late that evening, Ephraim came round to Bilbury Grange to see me.

'Thank you, doctor,' he said, smiling rather wanly. 'I didn't see that coming!'

'I thought it best that you didn't know what to expect,' I told him. 'Hope I wasn't too rough on you!'

'Oh no! It was brilliant. When you'd gone even Dicky said he wasn't going to do the jump. I think he was worried that he might end up in a wheelchair – or worse. Everyone in the shop thought you were terrifying and that I was very brave to have you as my doctor.'

'Jolly good!' I said. 'I think.'

Ephraim held out something to me. 'Since I'm not doing the parachute jump, I said I'd help the charity by selling these,' he said.

'What are they?'

'They're raffle tickets,' he said. 'Would you buy one, please? They're 10 pence each.'

'What can I win? Don't tell me I win a chance to make a parachute jump?'

'Oh no, nothing like that,' said Ephraim quickly. 'The prize is a pig, donated by a local farmer.'

I thought of Cedric, the pig we look after for its American owners: the pig which eats vast quantities of food and which produces a ton of manure every year.

The prospect of looking after two pigs was just too much.

'I tell you what,' I said, taking a 50 pence coin out of my pocket. 'I'll pay for five tickets but I don't want them. Don't give me any tickets. Just put the 50 pence into your collecting box.'

Ephraim looked surprised. 'Oh, all right, doctor.'

I gave him the 50 pence and bade him goodnight.

In the end, it all worked out quite well.

But I did make a mental note to go into a different shop the next time I went into Barnstaple for shoes or shoelaces.

I didn't want to wander in and find all the assistants rushing away from me in fear.

Sir Ebenezer's Statue

Visitors to Bilbury occasionally wonder why a small and unimposing triangle of land not 200 yards from the Duck and Puddle is adorned with a surprisingly impressive statue of an imposing looking man with a pipe in his mouth and a sword by his side.

Every village has these odd triangles of wasteland – too small to do anything with and usually suitable only for the erection of a signpost.

But I doubt if there is another village in England which has a full sized statue on one of its little triangles of unwanted land.

I doubt if many visitors to Bilbury know the true story behind the statue. So, here it is.

The story began when Cuthbert Potts, who sits on our Parish Council, decided that we ought to have a floral clock.

Cuthbert, who is obviously known to everyone as 'Chimney', said that places like Blackpool and Torquay have floral clocks and so he didn't see why Bilbury shouldn't have one.

He said that he thought it was terrible that Bilbury had neither a Jubilee Watering Trough (complete with dedication plaque and the word 'Horse' etched into the stone for the sake of literate equines) nor a floral clock, and that although he had no idea how to make a commemorative water trough he didn't think that making a floral clock could be too difficult.

It is true that at first, some of us weren't entirely sure that we actually needed a floral clock. After all, Bilbury doesn't go out of its way to attract visitors. Most of the tourists who wander into the village do so by mistake.

But Chimney said that he would create the clock himself and when he had a whip round to help pay for the cost of the bedding plants we all contributed according to our means.

And though it is true that we had not originally shown great enthusiasm, it is equally undeniable that there was much excitement during the months prior to the clock's unveiling.

As the weeks passed by, we became increasingly excited at the prospect of having our own floral clock. When we passed the site of the clock, many of us often stopped for a few moments and watched Chimney working away on his creation. Passers-by would say things like 'Look, it's twenty past a primrose' or 'Crumbs, it's nearly five to cyclamen!'.

In due course, notices were put up around the village inviting us all to the formal unveiling of Bilbury's first floral clock.

The official unveiling was fixed for 12.30 p.m. so that all those present could all repair to the Duck and Puddle afterwards for a champagne celebration. (The notice warned that only one bottle of champagne had been provided, courtesy of Frank and Gilly, the landlord and landlady of the Duck and Puddle respectively, and that additional supplies of alcohol would be available only at the expense of those present.)

And so at 12.30 p.m. on the appointed day, we were all there. Patsy and I were there. Miss Johnson was there. Frank and Gilly were there. Thumper and Anne were there. Patchy and Adrienne were there. A couple of dozen others were there too. It was quite a decent crowd. Maybe not the sort of crowd they get in London for a coronation or a royal wedding, but for Bilbury it was quite a decent crowd. There were even mumblings from some, who shall remain nameless, that we should have arranged for crowd barriers to be erected and for the local constabulary to have been invited to provide some sort of official protection detail. But these were, of course, remarks made in jest.

With a flourish, Chimney's wife and his mother lifted the tarpaulin from the clock. (They did it very gingerly to avoid damaging any of the blooms.) And then we stood and looked at the clock. It was, in many ways, a very fine clock. There is no doubt about the fact that it had been very nicely done. A good deal of work had been done in creating a clock out of small bedding plants. There was much to admire. No expense had been spared. The numbers 1 to 12 were made out of yellow primroses. The hands were made out of purple primroses. We all clapped and there is no doubt that we were proud of the clock.

The time according to the clock was 2.30.

We stood and waited and watched.

'It's telling the wrong time,' said Adrienne, looking at her watch. 'It's 12.15 but the clock says it's 2.30.'

'It'll be right in a little over two hours,' said Chimney, who seemed a little peeved at the complaint.

We stood around for a while. I don't know what we were waiting for, or what we expected to happen. The purple primroses clearly weren't going anywhere.

'Is it going? Can you wind it up?' asked Frank. 'Have you got the key?'

'What do you mean 'wind it up'?' asked Chimney. 'It's a floral clock. It's made of flowers.'

'He hasn't put a mechanism in it,' whispered Thumper, who was standing next to me.

I think we had all realised the problem with the clock at the same moment.

'It doesn't actually tell the time,' said Adrienne, who is not a tactful person by nature. She is the one person in the village who could be relied upon to tell the Emperor that he wasn't wearing any clothes. 'We've got a floral clock which doesn't tell the time!'

Chimney looked at her as if she were a one legged horse. 'Of course it doesn't tell the time!' he said. 'How can it tell the time? It's made of flowers.'

We all looked at one another. Slowly, it dawned on us that Chimney, bless him, hadn't realised that a floral clock is supposed to contain a mechanism so that it can tell the time.

Patchy looked at me and I looked at Thumper and Thumper looked at Frank.

None of us was prepared to tell Chimney that although his flower clock was a magnificent looking piece of ornamental horticulture, it was missing the one vital ingredient which would have set it off to perfection: a clock mechanism.

'I shall come here twice a day to check the time,' said Frank.

Gilly looked at him with her best 'you wait until I get you home' look. 'Three cheers for Chimney for creating a marvellous clock!' she said.

We cheered lustily.

And then we all retired to the Duck and Puddle to celebrate the clock's arrival in the village.

147

Unfortunately, the clock became famous, but not quite in the way that Chimney had hoped. Someone wrote a short piece of doggerel which was pinned up on the village notice board:

Bilbury has a floral clock
Those who looked tried not to mock
At half past two the clock was right
Whether it was day or night
Both men and women came from afar
In coaches and, of course, by car
They looked and stared without a laugh
At Bilbury's strange and well known gaffe

Things were made much worse when this rather cruel little rhyme appeared in the *North Devon Bugle*, a well-read local newspaper.

That was a while ago.

Within a year, the clock had pretty much disappeared. The weeds had taken over. You can still see the odd halves of one or two numbers if you know precisely where to look between the groundsel and the sheep sorrel, the buttercup and the stinging nettles, the hogweed and the hemlock, the cow parsley and the teasel.

And, if you look carefully, half of the minute hand can still be seen.

But Chimney had, not surprisingly, lost interest in his floral clock after the realisation that he had forgotten to include anything which would enable the clock to tell the time.

He had not, however, lost his feeling that Bilbury needed a focal point and he was tireless in his determination to put Bilbury on the map. One day in autumn he came into the Duck and Puddle and announced that what Bilbury needed was a statue.

'Why?' asked Patchy, not unreasonably. 'Why not an obelisk or a water trough with the words 'Horse Trough' chiselled into the stone in case anyone mistakes it for a boating pond for youngsters?'

'Everywhere has a statue!' said Chimney, who had clearly set his heart on a statue.

'We don't have a statue,' Frank pointed out. 'We're somewhere but we don't have a statue.'

Off the top of his head, Thumper then rattled off an impressive list of towns and villages in Devon which didn't have statues.

'All the more reason why Bilbury should have a statue!' said Chimney, who is not a man who is easily put off his stride.

'Who?' asked Frank.

'Who who?' asked Chimney.

'Who do we want a statue of? Or of whom do we want a statue?'

The pub fell silent while we all thought about this.

'Nelson,' said Chimney at last. 'Admiral Nelson.'

We looked at him.

'He's good enough for Trafalgar Square,' Chimney pointed out. 'So he should be good enough for Bilbury.'

'Was he born in Bilbury?' asked Thumper.

'Did he ever come to Bilbury?' asked Frank.

'Did he ever even come to Devon?' asked Thumper.

'Does it matter?' asked Chimney, defiantly. 'Without Admiral Nelson we would all be speaking Spanish.'

'I think I've got an old statue at the back of my workshop,' said Patchy suddenly.

Patchy Fogg, an antique dealer with an insatiable appetite for 'stuff', has at least one of almost everything you can think of tucked away at the back of his workshop.

We all looked at him.

'What of?' asked Chimney. 'Who is it a statue of?'

'Haven't the foggiest,' admitted Patchy.

'Is he on a horse?'

'No. But he looks very stern and he's got a sword. He's a very distinguished looking fellow with a slight military air to him. It's a decent looking bronze statue. And it will save us the trouble and expense of having one made.'

'But we can't just have a statue,' complained Chimney. 'It has to be a statue of somebody!'

'We could make something up,' suggested Frank, whose insurance claims are said to be such good works of fiction that a representative for a major insurance company suggested that he enter one year's claims for the Nobel Prize for literature.

'We couldn't possibly do that!' insisted Chimney, who can be a little straight laced at times.

This led to some silence.

'We should have a statue to General Sir Ebenezer Warwick,' I suggested, thinking I ought to say something useful.

'Who?' said Chimney.

'General Sir Ebenezer Warwick.'

'Who the devil was he?'

'Chap who was born in Bilbury and who fought in the Boer War. He was not well known, and he was ignored by history but he won loads of medals and led a famous, if rather unfortunate, charge at the Battle of Bloemfontein.' I turned to Patchy. 'Does your statue have a pipe?'

Patchy frowned. 'Don't think so.' He thought for a moment. 'No, no pipe.'

'We must give him one,' I insisted. 'General Warwick always smoked a pipe. Never went into battle without it. He would ride his horse at the head of a line of cavalry with clouds of smoke puffing out of his pipe. It must have been a marvellous sight.'

We all sat quietly for a few moments, contemplating General Warwick in full flight with a stream of tobacco smoke trailing behind him.

'We could get Reggie at the garage to make a pipe and then weld it on to the statue,' suggested Thumper.

'Perfect,' I said. 'And remember, he wasn't just a successful soldier. After the war he became a successful manufacturer of fine linoleums and high quality underlay. Linoleum was invented by an Englishman called Walton but it was General Warwick, the boy from Bilbury, who really put the stuff on the map. 'When they find themselves walking on our underlay, your feet will think they've died and gone to heaven' was one of the most popular slogans of the 19th century and Warwick was reputed to have written it himself. He had a huge factory in Walsall and was known to thousands as 'The Linoleum King'.'

'I remember hearing about him at school,' said Thumper, with a wise looking nod. The only things Thumper learned at school were acquired from lessons conducted behind the bicycle sheds.

'And he was a philanthropist too,' I continued. 'At every equinox he used to give offcuts of linoleum to the poor. For decades there wasn't a back-to-back kitchen in Walsall which didn't contain a free piece of linoleum, donated by the enormously generous General Warwick. Modern philanthropists make a big fuss about giving away a few quid and having a crematorium named after them but for them it's just a tax fiddle. General Warwick was a real philanthropist, driven by simple, honest-to-God generosity. The people loved him for it. When he died, the streets of Walsall were lined with mourners. I like to think that the people of Bilbury held a memorial service for their forgotten son.'

'But how do we know that Patchy's statue looks like this General Warwick?' asked Chimney whose lack of imagination is definitely a drawback in village life.

'No one alive knows what General Warwick looked like,' I told him. 'Not even the Imperial War Museum has any pictures of him. There are just the handwritten reports of him riding into battle with his pipe belching out more smoke than the Flying Scotsman. He has been sadly forgotten by the world. The Bloemfontein campaign is now considered by some to have been politically incorrect. '

'All the more reason why we should have a statue to commemorate his life,' said Thumper.

'So, that's agreed then, is it?' said Frank, who doubtless wanted the discussion over so that he could have his lunch. 'We get Reggie to weld a pipe onto Patchy's statue, stick on a label saying the statue is of General Thingy Warwick and plonk him down somewhere pretty central.'

'We could put him where the floral clock used to be,' suggested Thumper. 'We need something there, now that the clock has been overtaken by nature.'

That's what we decided.

And it is why, if you ever find the time and the inclination to visit our village, you will find that there is a large and very imposing statue of the immortal General Sir Ebenezer Warwick, complete with specially, hand-crafted pipe, peeping above the giant hogweed and the cow parsley on the corner of the unnamed lane leading down to Softly's Bottom.

Reggie at, Tolstoys, our local garage made the pipe and it was he who, with the crane on his breakdown truck, helped us to move the statue into position.

On warm, summer afternoons, Chimney can often be found loafing around in the vicinity of the statue.

And if someone passing through stops and asks for directions, as tourists often do, Chimney will, before he does anything else, insist on telling them the story of General Sir Ebenezer Warwick, a forgotten hero who led the famous charge at Bloemfontein and a man who bestrode the linoleum industry like a colossus.

Let no one say that we in Bilbury do not take our village history and our culture very seriously.

Charcoal and Geese

I first noticed Bevan Jeffrey early one morning when he was driving geese along the road that leads out of Bilbury and towards Barnstaple.

I didn't know who he was at the time; I'd never seen him before, but he was an imposing figure. From a distance, he looked to have been made at the same time as the pyramids, out of the same material and to the same sort of design; with strength, stability and an air of easy permanence taking precedence over folderols and artistic merit.

He was carrying a quarterstaff, the sort of weapon favoured by Little John, and he used it firmly, but with surprising gentleness, to nudge errant geese back into line. He wore an old black leather coat which came down to his calves and which had clearly seen much better days, though it doubtless still served its purpose, and there was a piece of blue baler twine wrapped round his waist.

I sometimes wonder how many miles of baler twine are used as fashion accessories in North Devon. The stuff, invariably bright orange or blue, is intended for use in binding up quantities of hay or straw, but in our part of the world, where it is relatively cheap and very easily available, it is used to fasten coats and to hold up trousers. It is used as shoelaces and, in windy weather, to hold on hats. I've even seen a woman using the stuff as a replacement strap for her handbag. The side view mirrors on Thumper's truck are both held in place with copious amounts of baler twine and I reckon that half the dog leads in North Devon consist of pieces of baler twine.

There seemed to be hundreds of geese in the flock being driven along the lane though in reality I doubt if there were more than three dozen. It's just that geese are very noisy, rather threatening birds and they move about a good deal. Whenever there are a few of them gathered together, it always seems that there are more of them than there actually are. Trying to count them must be a nightmare. If counting sheep is supposed to put people to sleep then counting geese must surely keep them awake. Sheep tend to stay in a flock, huddled together for security. Geese like to do their own thing.

I got stuck behind those darned geese for the best part of an hour. The road was just about wide enough for my car, so I couldn't turn round, and a tractor following behind me meant that there was no chance of my reversing away from the mobile blockage.

In the end, rather than pootle along behind the geese, and risk the inevitability of the engine overheating, I just parked the car, switched off the engine and read a book for a while. I never go anywhere without a paperback or a small, old hardback stuffed into a jacket pocket. Victorian and Edwardian publishers invariably produced hard books which were small enough to fit easily into a jacket pocket but these days travellers who want a book easily to hand have to rely on paperbacks. I can't remember the title of the book I had with me that day but I think it may have been one of H.V.Morton's travel books. Or maybe it was one of James Agate's magnificently gossipy 'Ego' diaries. As I settled down, I noticed that Willie, the driver of the tractor who was stuck behind me, had pulled out his copy of a tabloid newspaper. I'm not the only road user in Bilbury to travel around prepared to have to wait for the road to clear. It is, however, usually cows or sheep, rather than geese, which cause the blockage.

You don't often see a gaggle of geese travelling about these days but I know enough about country customs to be aware that geese driving used to be a common sight on English roads. Back in the 18th century, you couldn't go anywhere to see geese being moved from one place to another and it was common to see flocks of two or three thousand geese passing through towns and villages. The largest accumulation of geese ever seen was probably the drove of 9,000 which are said to have passed through Chelmsford in 1783. The geese in these huge flocks were built up a few at a time with geese being contributed by farmers and cottagers who wanted to send their birds to market.

I remembered reading somewhere that in 1740, an Englishman called Lord Orford made a big bet with the Duke of Queensbury 'that a drove of geese would beat an equal number of turkeys in a race from Norwich to London.'

Orford won the bet because his geese plodded steadily along the road which led to London whereas, as the evenings approached, the turkeys would fly up into the trees at the side of the road. And there they would insist on staying for the night. The drovers, responsible for moving them along, found it extremely difficult to get them down in the morning.

The result was that Orford's geese, which didn't stop to sleep, got to London two days earlier than Queensbury's turkeys.

Despite the delays on the roads, I sometimes think it is a pity that you don't see sights like that these days; maybe modern gamblers just don't have the style and imagination of their predecessors.

When I found myself stuck behind his flock, I didn't know that the man driving the geese was called Bevan Jeffrey and I didn't know anything at all about him.

But, purely by coincidence, I saw him again much later that day when I was driving in the opposite direction along the same stretch of road.

Since I had started running my own dispensary, a van came to Bilbury Grange every day with a delivery of essential drugs. But on this occasion I'd had to drive into the town to collect an oxygen cylinder and mask which had been sent on the last afternoon train to the local railway station. I had a patient with chronic bronchitis and emphysema who needed a home oxygen supply.

About half way back from Barnstaple, I saw a man striding along the road. The long leather coat was distinctive and I immediately recognised him as the fellow who had been driving the geese earlier that day. I stopped and asked if he wanted a lift back to Bilbury.

'How did you know I was heading for Bilbury?' he asked, when he'd settled into the passenger seat of the Rolls, and had admired the car.

He spoke in a surprisingly cut glass accent, in what used to be called BBC English, but there were no fancy airs or graces about him. He was not the sort of man I could ever imagine wearing spats or a flower in his buttonhole. His shirt probably never had a collar attached to it and if he ever wore a waistcoat there would probably be no shirt underneath it.

I told him that I'd seen him with his geese earlier in the day. 'I assume you were taking them into Barnstaple,' I said.

'It's market day,' he explained.

155

'It's a good long walk.'

'It's pleasant enough. And once you're used to them geese aren't too difficult to manage; surprisingly easy, in fact. I walk them into town because if I hired a lorry to take them into Barnstaple, the cost of the lorry, the petrol and the driver would take up most of my profit.'

He told me that it took about six hours to drive the geese to Barnstaple and that the walk back took him about three to four hours, depending on whether he stopped off along the way for refreshment.

As we drove back to Bilbury, he told me a lot about geese. I always enjoy listening to people talk about their work. And country folk always seem to have fascinating stories to tell about how they spend their days.

Bevan explained that geese are simple to manage and breed quite easily; a goose producing 12 to 16 eggs at a time and the eggs taking only around a month to hatch. He told me that he helped feed the goslings by giving them bread and milk and, later on by supplementing their diet with mash and grain. He said he fed the flock in the evenings and so he didn't ever have to worry about them coming home. He smiled when he told me that his geese always cleared up the windfalls in his small orchard and that later in autumn there were invariably one or two birds who ate too many of the over-ripe apples and became a little drunk.

'You don't keep them in some sort of pen?' I asked.

'No, I let them roam free in the woods where I live and work.'

He told me he had a cottage and five acres of woodland just a couple of miles away from Bilbury Grange. I knew the cottage. I had passed it hundreds of times, without realising who lived there.

'You don't have any trouble with foxes?'

He laughed. 'No! No fox would dare come near one of my geese. I've got one gander who would frighten away a bear let alone a fox.'

He told me that a gander is usually a good husband and father. 'They are usually very protective of their geese and goslings. I've seen a gander take a sitting goose to the pond for a swim and then get a spare goose, who had no eggs of her own, to sit on the eggs during the mother's absence.' He paused. 'I have a few swans who fly in occasionally. They seem to like being with the geese. They crossbreed occasionally. Do you know what we call the result of a mating between a goose and swan?'

I laughed and admitted that I didn't.

'It's a swoose! Honestly. A swoose.'

He said that the word came from a popular song called 'Alexander the Swoose' which had been written by a bandleader called Kay Kyser about a bird that was half swan and half goose. He confessed that he had only ever seen one swoose but that he knew a fellow in Hampshire who had bred quite a few of them. 'I sometimes wonder what their lifespan is,' he said. 'A swan can live to be 100-years-old but I've never heard of a goose living to much more than 20. Maybe a swoose manages somewhere between the two.'

He told me that he took a gaggle of geese to the market several times a year, that five times a year, when the geese moulted, he collected their flight and body feathers and sold them to a London buyer who used them for decorations, and that if he had what he thought was a glut of eggs he sold the eggs to local hoteliers and restaurateurs.

'I can't make a living out of geese alone,' he said, 'they're a bit of a sideline, and a pleasant one, but they contribute their share to my living expenses.' He said that the geese were also good company. He told me quite a bit about geese. It was Bevan who told me that although they are known as a gaggle when they're on the ground they're usually referred to as a team, a wedge or a skein when they're flying. And if they are flying close together they're known as a plump.

However, to my surprise Bevan told me that his main activity was charcoal making.

When I confessed that I didn't know there were still any charcoal makers still in business he told me that there was still a small but certain demand for charcoal and that if I wanted to see his charcoal making business I would be welcome at any time. I thanked him and said, quite truthfully, that I would be fascinated to see a charcoal burner at work.

'You don't come from round here, do you?' I said, when I'd stopped to drop him off at his cottage.

'The accent gives me away?' he said, with a laugh.

'It rather does.'

'Eton and Oxford,' he said, not boasting but simply explaining. 'Got a first in English. I used to have a job in public relations in London. Hated it. The damned job made me ill – gave me a stomach ulcer. It was an awful job which involved my being terribly nice to people I couldn't stand, but it paid well and at the time I thought that was important. Then my wife ran off, with our vicar actually, which was a bit of a shock to the system and made me look at my life a little more closely – what I was doing, what I wanted to do and so on. The sort of questions I'd never had time to think about let alone to try to answer. When we sold our flat and split the proceeds, I gave up my job and used the proceeds to buy the cottage down here. I didn't have the foggiest what I was going to do but I had enough money to last me six months. The previous owner of the cottage had at one time been a charcoal burner and since I didn't have anything better to do I thought I'd try my hand at it. The cottage came with a few acres of woodland which was pretty handy, of course.'

'I found it surprisingly simple, and a very pleasant change from what I'd been doing in London. It gave me plenty of time to read and study and to pursue my hobby of compiling crosswords.'

Bevan then told me that in addition to rearing geese and making charcoal, he also devised crosswords for *The Times* newspaper. He told me, without boasting, that he could create a complete crossword, complete with the grid, all the clues and the answers, in his head.

'So, you've got three jobs!'

He grinned. 'Pretty unusual combination, eh?'

I dropped him off, meaning to take him up on his offer to see how charcoal was made, but things were so busy for the next few weeks that I completely forgot the invitation.

The next time I saw him was about six months later.

He came to an evening surgery at Bilbury Grange and told me that he thought he had perhaps been made ill by his work making charcoal.

'Why do you think that?' I asked.

'What do you know about charcoal?' he asked in return.

'You can assume I know nothing.'

'It's a very old business. It would be pompous to describe it as a profession because the aim is simply to manufacture charcoal by carbonising wood in a kiln or a charcoal pile. Originally, people made charcoal because it could be burnt to produce the high temperatures required for smelting iron, glass making and a host of other industries. It's no longer used for that because other fuels are available, but there's still a market – making charcoal for suburban barbecues for example. Quite a few artists still use charcoal for drawing.'

I nodded to show that I was listening and understanding.

'Building a charcoal kiln is extremely simple. You arrange some logs in a conical heap and then build a sort of chimney in the middle and fill it with bits of kindling and brushwood. You then cover the whole thing, the kiln, with grass, moss and earth to keep the air out. You light the kindling in the middle of the kiln and the whole thing starts to slowly burn. The temperature goes up to about 300 degrees Centigrade and you have to control the amount of air going into the kiln by making holes and then sealing them up. The trick is to make sure that the wood is still on fire without allowing it to go up in flames. You can tell how well things are going just by looking at the smoke which comes out of the chimney in the centre of the kiln. When the smoke gets rather blue and thin then you know that you've nearly finished the process. Each kiln takes about a week. When you've finished you will, if all has gone well, have a nice pile of charcoal to sell.'

'It sounds hard work!'

'No, it isn't really hard work. It's more time consuming than it sounds because you have to hang around while the wood is burning. You don't want to waste all the wood. And you don't want the fire to go out. It's just a question of knowing how to control the burning.'

'So there's a lot of sitting around and waiting.'

'Precisely.'

'So that's when you create your crosswords!'

He laughed. 'You remembered!'

'I don't know anyone else who makes charcoal, breeds geese and writes crosswords!'

'No, I don't suppose there are many of us around.'

'So is all this dangerous? You think it's made you ill?'

'The problem is that making charcoal produces quite a lot of carbon monoxide.'

'And you think you might be suffering from carbon monoxide poisoning?'

He nodded. 'I've had the symptoms of it,' he said. 'When I started making charcoal I read a couple of books about it and the authors warned that it is possible to develop carbon monoxide poisoning from spending too much time in close proximity to the kiln.'

I asked him what symptoms he had.

'Tiredness, dizziness, nausea, confusion and feeling a bit faint,' he said. 'I also have difficulty breathing properly sometimes. And I've noticed that my heart seems to be beating unusually rapidly sometimes.'

'All of which are symptoms of carbon monoxide poisoning.'

'Exactly. Is there a test you can do?'

'I can take some blood and get it tested,' I told him. 'The laboratory people can measure the amount of carboxyhaemoglobin in your blood – a measurement of the amount of your haemoglobin that has bonded with carbon monoxide.'

I listened to his chest, checked his pulse and blood pressure and then took some blood and got it ready to send off to the laboratory in Barnstaple. I told him to come back to see me in a couple of days' time. Meanwhile, I suggested that he might be wise not to start a new kiln for a while.

But when the test result came back, Bevan didn't have any sign of carbon monoxide poisoning. There was no carboxyhaemoglobin in his blood at all.

'So, what do you think it could be?' he asked.

'I know what it is,' I told him. 'You're anaemic.'

'Anaemic!'

'Your haemoglobin levels are very, very low. And the symptoms of anaemia can be exactly the same as the symptoms of carbon monoxide poisoning: breathing problems, a rapid heartbeat, nausea, faintness, tiredness and dizziness.'

'But why on earth would I have anaemia? I eat well. Lots of meat, green vegetables and fruit.'

'That's what we need to find out,' I told him. 'I can treat your anaemia easily enough – just giving you some iron tablets will probably result in an improvement. But we have to find out why you are anaemic. It certainly doesn't sound as if your diet is short of iron.'

I asked him to undress so that I could examine him properly.

'What was this for?' I asked him, about a scar in his upper abdomen. I hadn't seen it when I'd listened to his lungs and heart and taken his blood pressure.

'I had a gastrectomy a few years ago.'

'What for?'

'For a stomach ulcer. I had a high pressure job which I hated. I ended up with an ulcer.'

I went back to my desk and picked up his medical records. 'There's no mention of it here?'

'My company paid for private medical insurance for me and the company doctor sent to me to a private specialist who organised everything.'

'They really should have sent a letter to your GP.'

'I think they liked to keep everything to themselves,' explained Bevan.

'Do you know what sort of gastrectomy it was?'

'I think the surgeon said it was a total gastrectomy.'

'For an ulcer?'

'Actually, I seem to remember them telling me that I had two or three ulcers.' He paused and smiled ruefully. 'I never have been one to do things by halves.'

'Did they tell you that you might need vitamin B12 supplements?'

Bevan frowned. 'I don't remember anyone mentioning that.'

'The stomach produces something called intrinsic factor,' I told him. 'And intrinsic factor is essential for the absorption of vitamin B12.'

'So I've not been absorbing vitamin B12 properly?'

'Probably not.'

'And could that cause the symptoms I've been having? The symptoms I thought were caused by carbon monoxide poisoning?'

'Vitamin B12 is essential for the production of haemoglobin,' I told him. 'So that's why you are suffering from anaemia. Removing your stomach meant that your body had no intrinsic factor. The absence of intrinsic factor meant that your body couldn't absorb vitamin B12 and the shortage of vitamin B12 resulted in anaemia.'

'Am I right in thinking that the doctors I saw should have realised all this? And should have warned me that I would need to take vitamin B12?'

'Er, well, yes,' I admitted.

I have never liked criticising other doctors but it is sometimes difficult to avoid criticism when doctors have been so egregiously incompetent.

'Can you give me some vitamin B12 tablets to take?'

'I could but they wouldn't help.'

'Why not?'

'Because without the intrinsic factor your body won't absorb the vitamin B12.'

'No, of course not. So what's the answer? Do I have to remain anaemic for the rest of my life?'

'No. Certainly not. I'll have to give you the vitamin B12 by injection. And then you'll need to have regular B12 injections.'

'For how long?'

'The rest of your life.'

'Oh. Is that all?'

'It should cure your anaemia,' I told him.

'Worth it then.'

'I think so.'

'When can I have the first injection?'

'I'll have the injection I need sent here tomorrow,' I told him. 'Come back tomorrow evening and I'll give it to you.'

'You're going to stick a needle in me?'

'I'm afraid I am.'

He took a deep breath. 'I hate needles but if it makes me feel better you can stick in as many needles as you like,' he said.

'One at a time will do the trick.'

He turned up a day later and I gave him the first of the injections which he would need to have for the rest of his life. He was kind enough to say that he hardly felt it. I have always found that when injecting into tissues such as muscle, rather than into a vein, the key to giving as painless an injection as possible is to jab quickly, squirt slowly and then move the tip of the needle round a little to reduce any possible swelling. Injections which are given tentatively always seem to cause more distress than injections which are given confidently and quickly.

Within a remarkably short time, Bevan Jeffrey was as fit as a fiddle.

Being a GP can sometimes be very satisfying.

I did get to see Bevan's charcoal kilns a week or so later. Patsy, who said she was interested, came with me. The charcoal making process was fascinating but I don't think we'll be going again. The geese hissed a good deal and chased us both around Bevan's stretch of woodland.

And yes, geese do bite.

Mrs Sinclair Returns

I hadn't seen Joyce Sinclair for two years when her daughter, Julia Johnstone, came bustling into my evening surgery. She was, I suspect, the sort of woman who bustled everywhere. She looked aggressive and she was aggressive.

'Do you remember my mother, Mrs Sinclair?' asked the daughter who was a very skinny, nervous sort of woman who never seemed able to keep still. She fidgeted constantly; playing with her earrings, her necklace, the buttons on her frock and the clasp of her handbag. I remembered that she was an administrator working for the council while her husband was (in Joyce Sinclair's memorable words) 'something big in sewage'.

I told Mrs Johnstone that I certainly did remember her mother.

Joyce Sinclair had been only 62-years-old when her daughter and son-in-law had insisted on putting her into a care home near Exeter. She was in the late afternoon of her life; still young enough to worry about overdue library books and the price of tea in China.

Joyce hadn't wanted to go anywhere. And I didn't see why she needed to. Indeed, I had pleaded with the daughter to let her mother stay where she was.

'She's comfortable in her own home,' I pointed out. 'She's got her own furniture and her own belongings – her books, her photograph albums, her ornaments. She seems to me to look after herself very well. She cooks good meals and her house is easy to manage. She's careful going up and down the stairs. The garden is small enough for her to manage. She knows all her neighbours. It's only a ten minute walk to the village shop. And I call in to see her once a fortnight. If she needs more help we can sort something out.'

'But she's getting to an age when things happen,' insisted the son-in-law who was big in sewage. He was hugely overweight and carried a folded copy of *The Guardian* newspaper as though it were a talisman. He looked like a particularly bad tempered version of one of those Old Testament Prophets; all wild grey hair and a grey beard long enough to fly about in the slightest of breezes. 'We'd never forgive ourselves if something happened.'

'Something terrible might happen,' said Mrs Johnstone.

'She might fall down the stairs,' said Mr Johnstone.

'She could very well fall down the stairs,' echoed his wife. 'Break a leg or a hip. Old people have very fragile bones.'

'Well, anyone could fall down the stairs,' I pointed out. 'And your mother isn't old. She's only 62. She could live another 40 years.'

'We think it's much better to arrange things as early as possible,' said Mr Johnstone. 'Before anything happens.'

'Silly to leave things until the last minute,' said Mrs Johnstone. 'Then everyone gets into a panic and things aren't done for the best.'

'We don't want any panic,' said Mr Johnstone firmly. He said this sternly, as though I had spoken out in support of panic.

'Old people can develop signs of dementia almost overnight,' said Mrs Johnstone.

'Oh no, I don't think so,' I said.

'Overnight,' said Mr Johnstone. 'I've heard of it happening. I read about a man who went to bed one night and woke up the next morning not knowing where he was.'

'Maybe he had a stroke?' I suggested.

'And that's another thing!' said Mr Johnstone. 'What if she had a stroke? With no one there. She lives alone, you know.'

'If you're worried about that then you install some sort of alarm system,' I suggested.

'Oh, I don't think we want to start down that road,' said Mr Johnstone.

'That's a long and rocky road,' said Mrs Johnstone.

'You'd have to knock down walls and put wires everywhere.'

'Mother would hate all that mess and trouble.'

'You don't have to knock down walls,' I pointed out. 'They make these alarm buttons that are connected to the telephone.'

'But what if she's unconscious?' said Mr Johnstone.

'Your alarm button wouldn't be much use then, would it?' pointed out Mrs Johnstone.

'She'll be much safer in a home,' said Mr Johnstone firmly. 'Somewhere properly run; with caring staff available day and night.'

I remember getting slightly dizzy as the pair continued their double act. Whatever one said the other would immediately leap in to endorse it. I really didn't like either of them.

In the end, of course, I could do nothing to stop Mr and Mrs Johnstone putting Joyce Sinclair into a nursing home.

Mrs Sinclair didn't want to go anywhere. She wanted to stay in her home. But she was frightened of her daughter and her grim husband. And by alternately bullying her and terrifying her, the pair succeeded in convincing her that she had to move. She seemed as powerless as I was to prevent the inevitable.

There was, of course, a reason for the Johnstones' determination to move Mrs Sinclair out of her home. And it wasn't concern for Mrs Sinclair's safety.

Through their connections with the local authority, the Johnstones had arranged for Mrs Sinclair to move into a council owned and run nursing home. Moreover, they had managed to fix things so that the council would pay for Mrs Sinclair's room and board.

And, naturally, the Johnstones had plans for Mrs Sinclair's cottage.

Within a day of moving her mother into the nursing home, Mrs Johnstone had arranged for a letting agent from Barnstaple to come out to Bilbury, to take photographs and measurements and to print up smart looking leaflets offering the property for rent to holiday makers. They'd arranged for a man from Barnstaple to come out and give the outside of the cottage a lick of paint. And they'd put up some new curtains too.

I had no proof that they were doing anything dishonest but I strongly suspected that the income from the cottage was going into their bank account rather than into Mrs Sinclair's account.

And Mrs Johnstone now seemed very much more smartly dressed than she had been when I'd last seen her. She was wearing a Rolex watch and carrying a handbag that looked as if it had probably cost a small fortune.

'How is Mrs Sinclair?' I asked.

Mrs Johnstone paused, as though not quite sure what to say. 'She won't see the official doctor,' she said, with some reluctance. 'She insists that she wants to see you. She's got quite difficult about it.'

She said this as though it were my fault, as though I must have somehow persuaded her mother to demand to see me.

'The official doctor?' I said, not quite sure what she meant.

'The nursing home has a doctor who looks after all the residents. He calls in once every month and signs prescriptions and so on.'

'What's wrong with your mother?' I asked.

'No one seems to know,' said Mrs Johnstone. 'She's put on a little weight and she seems to have gone downhill a bit recently.'

'I can't just pop in and see someone else's patient,' I explained.

'How about if we brought her to see you?' asked Mrs Johnstone.

'Not really,' I said. 'I could get into trouble. The establishment takes a dim view of doctors who poach patients.'

'I saw another doctor when we were on holiday in Scotland,' said Mrs Johnstone. 'I had a chest infection and I saw this doctor in Inverness. He gave me antibiotics.'

'That's different,' I said. 'If a patient is on holiday, he or she can see a doctor wherever they are in the United Kingdom.'

'There you are, then,' said Mrs Johnstone. 'I'll bring mother out to see you tomorrow evening. She can be on holiday in Bilbury for the day.'

This seemed to me to be stretching the rules paper thin but I didn't want to be awkward – particularly since Mrs Sinclair had asked to see me. 'OK,' I agreed. 'But when I have seen your mother I will need to write to the doctor who looks after her at the nursing home where she lives.'

'Oh, that's all right,' said Mrs Johnstone.

So, the following evening Mrs Johnstone turned up pushing her mother in one of those folding wheelchairs which can be fitted into a car boot. The two women were accompanied by Mr Johnstone. His hair and beard were longer than ever and he was still carrying a copy of *The Guardian* newspaper. For all I knew it could have been the same copy.

I could hardly believe the change that had taken place.

When I'd last seen her, Mrs Sinclair had been lively and very active.

She took long walks through the village and along neighbouring paths and bridle paths. She was perhaps a few pounds overweight, but nothing very much. Now she seemed to be seven or eight stones overweight. I wasn't surprised that she needed to be moved about in a wheelchair.

We said hello to each other.

'She's looking well, isn't she?' said Mr Johnstone.

I remembered that he was something big in sewage and wondered if he had some of his employer's product packed inside his skull instead of brains.

'Very fit,' said Mrs Johnstone.

'They feed the inmates very well,' said Mr Johnstone.

'Inmates?' I said, slightly puzzled.

'Residents,' said Mr Johnstone, correcting himself. 'The patients.'

'Oh.' I had always thought of inmates as people in prison. And there was no reason why people in a nursing home should be thought of as 'patients' unless they were actually ill.

I asked Mr and Mrs Johnstone to leave me alone with Mrs Sinclair so that I could talk to her and examine her.

'Oh we'll stay with her,' said Mrs Johnstone.

'Better if we stay,' said Mr Johnstone. 'The people at the nursing home think she might be developing dementia. She gets confused about things.'

I looked at Mrs Sinclair. She looked at her daughter and then at her son-in-law and then back at me. She shook her head so slightly that it was almost imperceptible.

'You can sit in the waiting room,' I said to the Johnstones. 'We'll call if we need you.'

'So, what's been happening?' I asked Mrs Sinclair when they'd gone. 'You've put on a little weight.'

'There's nothing to do but eat,' she said. She spoke slowly and indistinctly and sounded drugged. 'They won't let us go outside. Not even into the garden. We either sit in our rooms or in the lounge.'

'What's your room like?'

'It's about the size of a toilet cubicle and I share it with a man who had a stroke. He shouts and thrashes about all night. And he's very confused. Sometimes he tries to get into bed with me.'

She spoke very slowly and it took her a long time to tell me this.

'Have they got you on any drugs?' I asked. I remembered that Mrs Sinclair had always been a reluctant pill-taker and that when I had last seen her she had been on no medication at all.

She reached into her coat pocket and took out a piece of paper torn from a cheap notebook. She handed me the piece of paper. 'I got one of the nurses to write everything down for me,' she said.

I looked at the paper. It was immediately obvious why Mrs Sinclair sounded drugged. She was taking two different tranquillisers four times a day and a strong sleeping tablet every evening. She was also taking oral hypoglycaemics, used for treating type II diabetes mellitus and a variety of other drugs for heart disease and high blood pressure.

'Crumbs!' I said. 'How many pills do you take a day?' I started to add them up.

'Thirty seven,' said Mrs Sinclair. 'I counted them. Plus my vitamins.'

'Vitamins?'

'They like us to take vitamin tablets. They tell us they keep us healthy.'

'How many of those do you take?' I asked.

'They give us two every hour.'

'Two every hour! That's 24 a day.'

'The nurse in charge says that if one is good for us then two an hour must be better.'

I frowned but didn't say anything. It is widely assumed that vitamins are harmless. They aren't. Too much of a good thing can cause serious problems and can even kill. Some vitamins are water soluble and excess quantities can be excreted in the urine. But some are fat soluble and stay in the body – building up to toxic levels. And vitamins can sometimes interact badly with prescription drugs such as those which are used to treat heart and high blood pressure problems.

'What symptoms have you got?' I asked.

'I feel nauseous all the time. I have an upset tummy. And I have a rash I can't get rid of. They've given me creams but they don't help. I get tingling in my hands and feet and I get headaches too.' She paused and sighed. 'I never used to have headaches.'

'Can you undress and get up onto the examination couch?'

Mrs Sinclair pushed herself up out of the wheelchair and stood, still holding onto one arm of the chair. She was very shaky. 'If you help me.'

I helped her undress and climb up onto the examination couch.

There really wasn't anything much wrong with her. Her heart was beating too fast but it was regular. Her blood pressure was too low.

'Do I need all these pills?' she asked.

169

I looked at her for a while, wondering what to say. Doctors aren't supposed to criticise other practitioners. But I was too angry to care too much about protocol. It seemed that the nursing home where Mrs Sinclair was residing was definitely one of those places described as a 'happy tablet farm'.

'I don't think you need any of the stuff you're taking,' I told her. 'You need to lose a lot of weight and you need to start exercising again.'

'I want to come back home,' said Mrs Sinclair. 'Back to Bilbury.'

'Has your daughter sold your house?' I asked.

'No. They can't sell it without my permission. They're still renting it out to holiday makers. They do very well out of it.'

'Your daughter and her husband won't want you to leave the nursing home.'

'I know. But they can't stop me, can they?'

'No,' I said. 'They can't.'

'Will you tell them?'

'Do you want me to?'

'Yes, please.'

I helped Mrs Sinclair down off the examination couch and I helped her get dressed and settled back in the wheelchair.

And then I called her daughter and son-in-law back into the room.

'You've been a long time,' complained Mr Johnstone. 'The doctor at the nursing home sees thirty patients in the time you've spent on one.'

'He's probably much cleverer than I am,' I replied. 'I'm a bit slow sometimes.'

'Yes,' said Mr Johnstone. 'You wouldn't get any prizes for productivity, would you?' He looked at his watch, to drive home the point.

'Your mother wants to leave the nursing home and come back home,' I said.

If I'd said that she wanted to run away and join a circus the Johnstones could not have looked more shocked and appalled.

'Oh no, that's quite impossible,' said Mr Johnstone. 'Have you seen the state of her? She's physically incapable of looking after herself. And she's pretty well senile.' He said this with his mother-in-law sitting three feet away from him.

'Oh, I think she could manage quite well,' I said. 'If necessary, we could find a home-help in the village who could do things around the house.'

'No, no,' said Mrs Johnstone firmly. She looked at her mother and then at me. 'Whose idea was this?'

'I expect it was the doctor's idea,' said Mr Johnstone. 'Don't you doctors get paid according to the number of patients on your list?'

'We do,' I agreed.

Mr Johnstone turned to his wife. 'He just wants to boost his income,' he said. 'Greedy, bloody doctors. You can't trust them.'

'Just plain greedy,' said Mrs Johnstone. 'Taking advantage of a senile, old woman.'

'Your mother isn't senile,' I told her. 'And she wants to come back home.'

'Impossible,' said Mr Johnstone. 'We've let the house for the whole of the year.'

'Then I'm afraid you'll have to cancel the bookings.'

'Cancel? We can't do that.'

'I want to come home,' said Mrs Sinclair, very quietly.

'To whom does the house belong?' I asked her daughter.

'Technically, it's still mother's house,' admitted Mrs Johnstone, rather reluctantly.

'We can't cancel the bookings, and that's that,' said Mr Johnstone. 'And we both had to pull in a lot of favours to get mother into that nursing home.'

'Could I have a word with you outside?' I said to Mr Johnstone, who seemed to be the driving force in the relationship.

'No need,' he replied. 'No secrets here.'

'OK,' I said. 'May I ask who gets the money from the rentals?'

Mr and Mrs Johnstone looked at each other.

'I don't think that's any of your business,' said Mr Johnstone.

'Maybe, maybe not,' I said. 'But if the income from renting Mrs Sinclair's home has been going into your account that could seem like fraud to some people.'

Mr Johnstone went very pale.

'Who's been paying the income tax on it?'

Mr Johnstone went even paler.

'I really do think your mother would be much better off if she were at home,' I told Mrs Johnstone.

171

Mr and Mrs Johnstone looked at each other. They leant together and there was some whispering. I busied myself unnecessarily with some papers on my desk and then started to make some notes about Mrs Sinclair's medical condition.

'If you really think mother would be better off at home then that's what we want too,' said Mr Johnstone.

'Perhaps some of the rental income you've received could be used to put a stairlift into the cottage,' I said. 'It would help until Mrs Sinclair loses some of that weight she's gained.'

They said they thought that could be managed.

And so it was agreed.

Two weeks later Mrs Sinclair was back living in her cottage in Bilbury.

Within two months, she was free of most of the tablets she was taking, though still cutting down the addictive tranquillisers she had been given. And she had started to lose weight and begun walking, very slowly, around the village again. A change in diet, and a reduction in weight, meant that Mrs Sinclair no longer needed to take drugs for her type II diabetes which was now almost cured. And we'd found a home-help (whose wages the Johnstones had, with some initial reluctance, agreed to pay).

Being a lone GP in a rural practice can sometimes be tiring, lonely and even frightening. Support may be an hour away or, in bad weather, impossible to reach.

But sometimes being a country GP can be exceptionally satisfying.

It was a joy to have Mrs Sinclair back in the village.

Sporting Heroes

My friend Will, who is a GP in the Midlands, has some glamorous and famous patients. He looks after a television presenter who reads the news on a local station and an actress who appears regularly in a soap opera.

But it is the sports stars on his list of patients who have proved most challenging – probably because they are the highest profile and the most valuable in raw commercial terms.

Six months ago, a patient of Will's who plays football for a leading club was about to be transferred to another team when a routine medical, performed by a doctor acting for his new club, showed that the player had a heart problem.

There was much panic. The team which was buying the player's contract decided that they wouldn't go ahead with the purchase. The team which was selling the player announced that they would take legal action. The player, who was naturally upset by the revelation, frightened everyone by talking of early retirement. The player's personal manager threatened to sue the doctors who had made the diagnosis. And the media had a field day.

Will was involved because he was the player's GP.

'Why didn't you spot this?' the club manager demanded.

Will pointed out that the heart problem, which was so mild that it might well have been better for everyone if it had remained undiscovered, had only been found after the player had been subjected to an angiogram – a fairly complex and high risk investigation which is usually only performed when a patient has symptoms of heart disease.

The player had absolutely no symptoms, and tests on the pitch and in the laboratory showed that he was perfectly capable of satisfying the significant physical demands of his profession. Every test showed that he was, in fact, one of the fittest and healthiest players in the League.

Eventually, the player solved the problem by announcing that he wanted to stay with his existing club and that he definitely didn't want to move to the club which had questioned his health.

Will was unhappy because he felt that there had never been any need to subject his patient to such an invasive procedure. Angiograms, which involve pushing a tube through a vein into the heart, are dangerous procedures which result in a number of deaths every year. Will felt that the abnormality which was unearthed was trivial and of no practical significance and that if the same level of examination was applied to other workers no one would ever be declared fit for employment of any kind.

Another patient of his, a well-known and moderately successful tennis player, arrived at Will's surgery one day carrying a form for an insurance company medical. The player had for years carried insurance to cover him against accidental damage to a limb, and the company which provided the cover had decided that it was time that they had another medical report so that they could evaluate their risk.

Unfortunately, when Will performed the medical, he found that the player (who like many professional sportsmen, had a very slow resting pulse rate, in his case of 32 beats a minute) had some very strange symptoms – particularly since he was a professional athlete who was expected to be super fit. He had an irregular heartbeat, rapid breathing, poor balance and decreased reflexes.

It turned out that the player, who suffered from the symptoms of an ulcer, almost certainly brought on by the stress of knowing that his ability to progress far enough through tournaments to earn a living depended on his winning his next match, had for months been treating himself with a proprietary brand of antacid which contained fairly large quantities of calcium carbonate and magnesium. The symptoms he was showing were all caused by the medicine he had bought over the counter. Many people assume that medicines bought from a pharmacy or a supermarket cannot possibly be dangerous but, sadly, that is not the case. If you take too much of anything the results can sometimes be catastrophic.

Will had to write a letter to the player's own doctor, explaining the situation and recommending that a safer treatment for the ulcer problem be provided. He also had to tell the player that he wouldn't be able to renew his insurance policy.

Bilbury doesn't have any high profile sporting residents (though we do have our fair share of celebrities, mostly retired, from the entertainment business) but that doesn't mean that I do not sometimes find myself dealing with amateur sportsmen who have medical problems.

And, as I have frequently discovered, amateur sportsmen and sportswomen can suffer just as much as the professionals. The amateur player may take his game just as seriously as the professional.

I have, for example, seen a number of patients with what I call 'skittle bowler's elbow', some with 'skittle bowler's shoulder' and several with 'skittle spectator's ankle'. The first two disorders are caused when a player hurls his skittle with too much force – or plays too many games. The third disorder is caused when an inattentive spectator does not see the heavy wooden ball used in skittles jump the boards at the side of the alley before bouncing out into the spectating area.

Ten pin bowling, the modern, domesticated version of the sport which is popular in the United States, is much safer in that spectators aren't allowed to stand around in the direct line of fire.

In a traditional skittle alley, there are invariably spectators linking up alongside the alley itself and when a ball bounces over the low wooden wall (as it invariably does at least once or twice in an evening) it is almost certain that someone will be hit. Indeed, I have, on two separate occasions, seen spectators injured by flying skittles. I bet that's an injury that is completely unknown in ten pin bowling!

And I will never forget that in 1970, a girl called Beatrice Jones insisted on a trial for Bilbury's rugby team.

Beatrice, who weighed just over 14 stone, was a big girl in every department and when she ran, she bounced a good deal. Indeed, there were parts of her which didn't stop moving for a minute or so after she had stopped running. She was luxuriously upholstered by a God who had chosen not to stint in any of the popular departments. She was also as tough as a rhinoceros. If she had chosen to be a boxer instead of to play rugby, she would have fought as a heavyweight and there would have been much trembling of the knees among all other contenders.

Since a rugby team needs 15 players and there were only 14 playing members in the Bilbury rugby club, the trial was something of a formality.

'Can you walk about under your own steam?' asked the team captain, who was also the selector and groundsman.

Beatrice said that she could.

'Can you catch a ball?'

Beatrice said she could do that too.

'Good, you're in the team.'

'I will play in any position except hooker,' she told him firmly, for she was a sensitive girl who did not wish to see her family embarrassed by seeing their daughter described as a hooker on the sports pages of the local paper.

The captain was doubtless happy to have found his 15th player but her inclusion resulted in much discussion, some controversy and, at first at least, a good deal of merriment.

Opposition players wanted to know how and whereabouts they should tackle her. Which did she prefer: above or below the waist? When she threw the ball in for lineouts there were complaints that not all of her body was behind the line. On one occasion, opposition players, theoretically there as defenders, stood mesmerised as she ran towards them, turned and watched agape as she ran past them and then stared motionless as she ran on to the line to score a memorable try. She was the heaviest player on the pitch and apart from not knowing precisely where to tackle her without offending the bounds of public morality, opposition players were wary of taking her on lest they find themselves simply being towed behind an unstoppable force. No red-blooded young male wants to be seen being towed along by a female rugby player.

Attempts were made to have her banned but the league administrators eventually reported that they could find nothing in the rules to stop her playing.

And the controversy didn't end when matches finished.

Since it was clear to players, officials and management that she could not possibly be expected to share the team bath, the captain decided that she should be allowed to take her bath first.

After standing in the rain for 25 minutes waiting for Beatrice to finish using the facilities the rest of the team rebelled, marched into a changing room smelling of lavender and plunged into a large bath of water which was now tepid and smelling of rose water. Beatrice, who was inadequately wrapped in a hand towel and busy doing her hair, refused to leave until she'd finished titivating. When the team wives and girlfriends found out about this incident, a delegation marched on the club president's home and demanded action. They weren't quite sure what sort of action they wanted but they wanted some of it and they wanted it fast.

In the end, disaster was averted only when Beatrice announced that she was pregnant and that she and the full-back would be marrying as soon as the season was over and a Saturday afternoon would be available for the necessary ceremony and celebrations. The full-back was at least six inches shorter than his bride-to-be and four stones lighter. She felled an opposing team member who said something rude about him; floored the man with a single punch.

The full-back said that he would continue playing but that his wife was retiring from competitive rugby due to her condition. Beatrice told a reporter from the local newspaper that she believed that in due course women would be playing rugby regularly and that in order to accommodate this eventuality, clubs would have to provide extra bathing facilities. She said she could see the day coming when there would be rugby and football teams made up entirely of women. No one was rude enough to say that they did not take her prediction seriously but it was generally agreed that it was an unlikely prospect since, as one club member put it, 'they don't make rugger boots small enough for women'.

Of course, the saga of the female rugby player wasn't my problem. It was a social and sporting dilemma rather than a medical one.

But other sporting difficulties did come within my remit and during one short week period I saw two local sporting stars who needed help or advice.

First up came Charles Crowcombe; a mountain of a man who was known to everyone as Charlie.

I think it was safe to say that Charlie was a character. He was so much of a character that I cannot imagine how I have managed to write eleven other books about Bilbury without once mentioning him. Charlie was 79-years-old and as full of beans as a cheap hotpot. He was a big man in every sense of the word and if there were a lion anywhere running around without a heart then Charlie had that missing organ.

I think the phrase 'larger than life' was invented for him.

The first thing that struck you about him was that he had a giant forehead. It always seemed to me that this was a bit of a fraud because it suggests, quite falsely, that great quantities of brain lie hidden behind it. In truth, the bony edifice reminded me very much of one of those fake fronts which Hollywood used to favour as a cheaper alternative to building a saloon, a row of shops or a chateau. 'Just build the front and don't let anyone peep around the sides.' Charlie had a big forehead but there wasn't much of anything on the other side of the bone.

I can still remember when I first met Charlie.

He came into the surgery because he had stuck a fork into his foot and needed a little light repair work. He refused point blank to go to the hospital in Barnstaple so I ended up dealing with the injury myself. Fortunately, he made a good recovery and there was no permanent damage.

(I am, incidentally, amazed at how many people stick forks into their feet. If more farm workers and gardeners wore stout boots, the world would be a safer place for feet.)

That was three years earlier than the problem which I now remember as 'the darts incident'.

'I'm 76-years-old,' I remember Charlie telling me with a fierce sparkle in the eye that didn't have the cataract. 'I have a long family history of heart disease. Both my parents died of heart trouble. I had three brothers and they all died of heart trouble. I eat four rashers of bacon and three eggs for breakfast every morning and I've done that since I was 16-years-old. I eat steak three times a week. I drink five pints of beer every evening and smoke 40 cigarettes a day – the ones without the girly filters stuck on the end. You may be able to conclude from this that death is not something I worry about a great deal. And nor do I take much notice of you medical people. I had a cousin called Earnest who was a keen athlete and a dedicated vegan. He never touched booze or cigarettes and never ate fatty food. He ate one egg a week but only the white bit. He wouldn't eat ice cream or chocolate but ate vast amounts of kale and spinach. Despite all this, he had a heart attack while out jogging. He was just 44 when he died. What sort of life was that for a fellow to live? He left a wife and a white poodle that had a pink collar. I had another cousin called Victoria who was knocked off her bicycle when she was 32-years-old. She used to cycle 200 miles a week. She broke a leg, had a fat embolus in hospital and died. My wife, God bless her, was a good woman. I loved her dearly. She made the best pies and I always had seven clean shirts a week. Nine years ago, she went into hospital for what they said was a routine operation down below. They were going to take everything away and send her home to me a bit lighter but as good as new. She never came home. She had the operation but she died. I never knew why. No one told me and I didn't ask. It didn't matter, did it? It didn't make any difference. She was a healthy woman, other than that bit of feminine trouble she had down below. So don't tell me to change my diet or to go to the hospital because I won't do either; not for you and nor for anyone else.'

So, I cleaned up his foot, scraped out the bits of shoe and sock and dirt that had got into the wound, courtesy of the fork prongs that had skewered him, sewed him up, gave him antibiotics and prayed that he would heal successfully. Fortunately, he did.

When he came back to have his dressing changed, I offered him an appointment with an eye specialist for the cataract. He looked at me as if I'd suggested he might like to adopt a vegetarian diet and shook his head pityingly as he hobbled off.

Charlie has a good many hobbies.

He is too slow to play football for more than five minutes at a time but he still coaches the village team. In matches he acts as a linesman, though he usually sits on a chair positioned in the middle of the touchline, rather than running up and down as the play ebbs and flows.

He has a small boat which he keeps in Combe Martin and he fishes regularly for mackerel. He catches more than he can possibly eat and he sells the rest to Peter Marshall who sells them on to a fishmonger who had a shop in Combe Martin. (I never understand why Charlie didn't just sell the fish direct to the fishmonger.)

And he plays darts.

Actually, to say that Charlie plays darts is like saying that Arnold Palmer, Jack Nicklaus and Gary Player played golf. Or like saying that Rod Laver and Ken Rosewall played tennis.

Charlie may have other interests but he lives for darts. It is his passion.

And, despite the cataract, he is very good at it, too.

He has been a member of the Duck and Puddle darts team since the team had been founded and when the team sheet is pinned up on the noticeboard, his name is always top of the list. This may, of course, have something to do with the fact that he is President, Chairman and Secretary of the darts club and captain and sole selector of the team. If there were a treasurer he'd be treasurer too.

Bilbury doesn't have a lot of league or cup winning teams.

Neither the cricket team nor the football team has had a great deal of competitive success. But our darts team has won so many trophies that they are stacked two deep in a specially made display cupboard standing at the back of the snug at the Duck and Puddle. Admittedly, some of the trophies had to be purchased by the darts team players themselves because in some of the tournaments where they were victorious, the organisers didn't have any money to pay for a trophy. (From time to time, the players had purchased second-hand trophies. And so the cabinet contained one trophy awarded to the Winners of the South West of England Netball Championship and another originally awarded to the winner of the Ladies' Match play Championship at the Kentisbury Golf Club.) But a trophy is a trophy is a trophy, as Gertrude Stein would have doubtless said if she'd thought of it or been interested in darts, and all the trophies in the cupboard had been won fair and square.

So when Charlie turned up in my surgery and told me that he was having a problem in letting go of his darts, I had to take him very seriously.

It was not a problem I had encountered before and I had to ask him to explain what he meant.

'When I've got the dart in my hand, like this,' said Charlie, picking a pen up off from the desk and holding it like a dart, 'It seems to stick to me. I can't let go. It's just like it's stuck to my fingers.'

'Ah,' I said.

'Ah,' is what doctors always say when they don't have the foggiest idea what is going on.

I am pretty sure that they never taught us about sticky darts at medical school but they didn't teach us about 'Ah,' either. That comes naturally. There is no exclamation point after it, by the way. That would be a very different sort of 'Ah'.

'How long has this been going on?' I asked.

'Three weeks,' replied Charlie as though this were a lifetime and a half. 'It started during a league match against King George. It got worse when we played King Charles. And last week, when we played Duke of York I could hardly let go of the dart. It's messing up my timing and my accuracy has gone all to pot.'

'Those are all pub darts teams?'

'They are.'

'Let me see your hands?'

He showed me his hands. They didn't seem to be unduly sticky. I didn't want to spend hours trying to find out why he couldn't let go of his darts and then find out that his fingers were covered in a thin but still sticky layer of all-purpose glue. Charlie used to be a carpenter and it was he who made the trophy cabinet in the Duck and Puddle. He still does a little sawing and hammering and doubtless messes around with the sort of glue that is nigh on impossible to remove. Personally, I hate it when my hands get sticky. There's nothing worse than examining a patient and finding after a couple of moments that your fingers are firmly stuck to whatever part of them you were palpating.

Charlie paused and frowned; deep furrows appearing across his massive, bony forehead. 'Do you think I might have been thinking too much?' He said this as though he were embarrassed by the very thought; as another man might ask if I thought he might have been smoking too much or drinking too much or eating too many chips.

I told him that we might have to consider this as a real possibility.

'Do you practise?' I asked. I know there are some sportsmen, usually not very good ones it has to be said, who regard practising as a form of cheating. I should have guessed that Charlie wasn't one of them.

'Of course I do!'

'And what happens when you practise? Can you let go of the dart?'

'No problem at all, doc,' said Charlie firmly. 'I can throw a mean dart when I'm practising. But when it's a competition, the darts go all over the place. I missed the board and hit the wall twice the other week. The other team were all laughing at me.'

Charlie was not, I suspected, a man who found it easy to be the butt of someone else's mockery.

'The more I try to deal with the problem the worse it gets. I concentrate hard, really hard, and when I eventually manage to let go of them the darts just fly off as though they have minds of their own. One stuck in a woman's foot last Friday. Fortunately she was a bit tiddly and she laughed so much that she didn't get cross.'

'Ah,' I said again, speaking as much to myself as Charlie. 'So it's a psychological problem rather than a physical problem.'

It didn't seem likely that Charlie had a physical problem, a neurological problem for example, if he could throw darts when it didn't matter. The fact that the problem only arose under pressure was quite a clue.

Charlie frowned. 'A psychological problem?'

He paused, and frowned, and half closed his eyes and repeated it, playing with the word as though it were something he'd come across but couldn't quite remember where or why.

'Psychology? That's to do with the head isn't it? The inside of the head?'

'It is,' I agreed. 'It's to do with what goes on in the mind.'

He looked at me rather suspiciously. 'Are you saying I'm off my trolley, doc? Ready for the loony bin?'

'No, no,' I said quickly. 'I'm just saying that the problem is clearly in your head rather than in your hand.'

Charlie kept his frown in place. 'What does that mean?'

'It means that we have to find out what's changed,' I said. 'Something is clearly putting you under extra stress.'

'I don't suffer with stress,' said Charlie immediately, firmly and irrevocably. He shook his head as though to confirm this. 'Never have, never do, never will. I've heard of it. There was an article about it in the paper. People in London get stress. People with suits and briefcases. Not me. Stress is for namby pambies.' He scowled at me. 'Are you saying I'm a namby pamby? '

'No,' I said quickly. 'Of course not.' Charlie may be a septuagenarian but he is a large septuagenarian.

'So, if it's not stress, what is it? What's wrong with me?'

I thought for a moment. 'I suspect that idiopathic muscular tension is impeding your flechette release mechanism,' I told him.

'Oh,' said Charlie, appeased. He seemed quite impressed. Actually, I was pretty impressed too. 'Would you write that down for me, doc?'

I tried to remember my diagnosis, carefully wrote it all down and handed him the piece of paper on which it was written.

Charlie looked at it and tried to say it. He didn't do very well. 'So that's what you think it is?'

'That's definitely what it is.'

'Can you cure me, doc?'

'Of course I can,' I said.

It seemed to me that I would never be able to cure Charlie's problem unless he believed I could cure his problem. In circumstances like this, confidence is all.

'You can give me some tablets?'

'No,' I said. 'I don't think tablets are necessary.'

I had a few weeks earlier read about a book in which the author suggested that most skilled sportsmen rely upon muscle memory to achieve success and that extraneous thoughts can interfere with the ability of the muscles to do what they have been trained to do. It was, I think, a new theory but to me it made complete sense. The author of the article suggested that whether they play golf, tennis or billiards, sportsmen or sportswomen do their best when they don't allow their conscious mind to interfere too much with what their hands, arms, legs are doing. I didn't see why this theory shouldn't apply just as well to darts.

'When is your next match?'

'We've got a home match next Wednesday. We're playing The Gravedigger's Rest.'

'You have to learn to stop concentrating on what you're doing,' I told him. 'You're trying too hard and as a result your muscles are becoming tense. That's why you can't let go of the dart.'

'How do I not try too hard, doc?' asked Charlie, puzzled. He was, I suspect, a man who always tried too hard.

'When you're about to throw your dart you have to concentrate on something else.'

'You mean, not concentrate on the shot?' Charlie seemed sceptical.

'Exactly,' I told him.

'So what do I concentrate on?'

'Concentrate on your breathing,' I told him, after a moment's thought. 'Tell your arm where you want the dart to land and then forget about the process of throwing the dart. Your body can manage that part perfectly well without your brain interfering. Instead of concentrating on hitting the triple twenty or whatever it is, just concentrate on taking slow breaths. Tell yourself to breathe in. And then tell yourself to breathe out. Do that just before you throw the dart and right up until the moment when the dart leaves your hand.'

Charlie looked at me as if I had gone mad.

'Really,' I told him. 'Try it. What have you got to lose?'

He thought for a moment. 'Not a lot,' he admitted.

The following Wednesday I made sure that I was at the Duck and Puddle for the darts match.

When it was Charlie's turn to play, I couldn't help noticing that the spectators, the members of the other team, and even the members of his own team, tried to stand behind him. They obviously all knew of Charlie's problem and thought that they would be safer there. One or two of the visiting team called out comments and advice to one another. 'I wish I'd borrowed a suit of armour from the museum!' 'Put your hands over your private parts when he throws!' 'Shall we go outside and watch through the window?' and 'Watch out for the ricochets!'

Charlie, it was clear, was not taking this well. His face was red and he was perspiring heavily. I couldn't help thinking about the family history of heart disease, the daily eggs and bacon and all those steaks.

Charlie's first attempts were a disaster. He was clearly still having difficulty in letting go of his darts. And when he did finally manage to launch them on their journey, he was hurling them towards the board as though he wanted to get rid of them. None of them stuck in the dartboard. They all bounced back quite a distance.

When he moved away from the oche, the line on the mat where players stand when it is their turn to throw their darts, I moved over to him, grabbed his elbow and led him away from the crowd of spectators and other players.

'I did the breathing thing like you said!' complained Charlie. 'But when I looked at the board I found myself thinking about the last match I played, when that dart hit that woman's foot.'

'So, the next time it's your turn, you must shut your eyes before you throw your darts.'

'Shut my eyes? So that I can't see?' Charlie sounded incredulous. I nodded.

So he did. He didn't score well but he managed to let go of all three darts and they all hit the board point first and stayed where they had landed.

'Next time, concentrate on your breathing and just squint a bit,' I told him. 'Almost close your eyes – but not quite.'

And, to his delight and astonishment, his darts all went where they were intended to go. I was delighted and astonished too.

I didn't tell him this, of course, but I think that having to concentrate on breathing and on almost closing his eyes meant that he didn't have enough brain left to worry about what he was doing.

After that, Charlie soon got back to his winning ways. It had all been a little unorthodox, to say the least, but it had worked. With his return to form, the Duck and Puddle team succeeded in defeating the team from the Gravedigger's Rest.

'Thanks, doc,' said Charlie afterwards. 'And it's good to know that my problem wasn't caused by stress. Not like one of those namby pamby types in suits, eh?'

Later, as the team celebrated, I heard one of the other players ask Charlie what his problem had been. Charlie took out the piece of paper on which I had written the diagnosis and everyone in the pub looked at it and nodded wisely, as though they understood what it meant.

That did make me smile.

My second sporting patient had a more serious problem in that it affected his health and, it is no exaggeration to say, threatened his life.

Farley Woodbury was 42-years-old when his wife, Petronella, brought him to see me.

Farley is a shy, quiet man; not the sort of fellow who ever rushes into things.

He certainly didn't rush things when he was courting Petronella, the daughter of a dentist in South Molton. She had a couple of horses of her own which she rode at meetings and they met at a Point to Point meeting held on a farm just outside Bideford. Petronella once told me that she and Farley were courting for three weeks before they progressed to Christian name terms. And it was another three weeks before they held hands in the back row of the cinema in Boutport Street in Barnstaple. Farley and Petronella went out together for two years before he proposed –once again in the back row of the cinema in Barnstaple. Petronella once told me, with some pride, that Farley still had the tickets stubs from that important evening and that he kept them in a matchbox in the top drawer of the bedside table on his side of their bed. It was not until eighteen months after the engagement that they married. Once married, Farley moved out of the accommodation he shared with two other single labourers, and Petronella left home. They moved into a small, tied cottage owned by my father-in-law and provided for married employees.

As a couple, they are a strange reversal of nature's usual allocation of colours. The male peacock is far more flamboyant than the female. The male pheasant is the one who has the flashy tail. But with Farley and Petronella, things were the other way around. She always wore bright, primary colours while he invariably wore earthy colours – dark greens and dark browns.

Although he works as a labourer on my father-in-law's farm, Farley has been a keen amateur jockey since his teens. He originally had hopes of becoming a professional jockey but he is nearly six feet tall and he finds it nigh on impossible to get down to the weights required by owners and trainers.

Jockeys who appear at National Hunt meetings, where nearly all the races are over fences, are allowed a little more leeway than flat race jockeys but a jockey's weight is still a vital factor in deciding whether or not he is given enough rides to make a living out of the sport of King's.

Farley's constant struggles with his weight meant that he had to abandon all his hopes of a career as a professional and, instead, to embrace the idea of a more modest career as an amateur jockey, racing very occasionally at larger meetings and quite often at Point to Point meetings where the requirements are slightly less stringent.

The problem was that as he grew older, Farley found it more and more difficult to get down to the weight required for even these lesser meetings. Professional jockeys sometimes spend hours sitting in a sauna in order to lose weight and it was not at all unknown for some to take amphetamines or other drugs to help them get down to the required weight. Neither of these options was available to Farley. He had a full time job as a farm labourer and couldn't afford the time to spend hours sitting in a sauna. On a farm labourer's wages, he couldn't afford the money to pay for illegal drugs.

'There's something wrong with Farley,' said Petronella.

Farley sat beside her, on the other side of my desk, and examined his fingernails.

I normally prefer patients to talk to me about their health problems but I knew that Farley was probably too shy to tell me anything so I allowed Petronella to speak for him.

'What sort of something?'

'He's losing a lot of weight.'

'How much weight has he lost?' I asked.

'A stone,' replied Petronella. 'He's always been terribly skinny but now he's just skin and bones.'

'How much do you weigh now?' I asked Farley, speaking to him directly for the first time.

'A little over ten stone,' replied Petronella. 'And that's when he's fully clothed and soaking wet. At a race ten days ago he weighed in at exactly ten stone.'

'And how tall are you?'

'Six feet two inches.'

'How is your appetite?'

'He eats very well,' said Petronella. 'He's not eating any less than he was. In fact I don't think I've ever known him eat more.'

'But you're losing weight?'

'A stone in the last six weeks,' said Petronella.

'Do you have any other symptoms?' I asked him.

Petronella looked at him and this time Farley did speak. 'No,' he said, without looking up.

There was clearly something more than I could see going on here. If Farley was eating properly but losing weight at such a dramatic rate then there was something seriously wrong with him.

Unless.

There was, I realised, another possibility.

Farley was a jockey and jockeys are always fighting to lose weight. Some lose weight by spending time in a sauna. Some take drugs. But there is another, very effective, way to lose weight which is often used by jockeys. If Farley was using this method then it seemed clear that Petronella didn't know about it and hadn't guessed what he was doing. Before I did anything else I needed to talk to Farley alone.

'I need to examine you,' I said to Farley. 'Take your clothes off and jump onto the examination couch.' I turned to Petronella. 'Would you pop back into the waiting room for a few minutes?'

She didn't want to go. I understood and sympathised. But I needed to talk to Farley without his wife by his side.

'So, is there anything else you should tell me?' I asked Farley when he was lying on the examination couch and his wife was out of my consulting room and back in the waiting room. Wearing just his socks and underpants he looked like a skeleton.

'No, I don't think so,' said Farley, so quietly that I could hardly hear him.

I examined him carefully. Inside his mouth, I could see the marks made by his fingernails. On the backs of his knuckles, I spotted the tell-tale sign where his skin had rubbed against his incisors. The skin on the back of his hands showed that he was seriously dehydrated. And when I listened to his heart I found that it was beating abnormally. I didn't need any more evidence.

'How long has it been going on?'

'What?'

'Making yourself sick.'

'I don't know what you're talking about,' said Farley, defiantly.

I looked at him and said nothing but just waited.

Suddenly he started to cry.

'It's my last chance,' he told me.

I waited.

'I've been offered a ride at the Cheltenham Festival. A trainer I know has offered me a ride if I can make the weight he wants me at.'

'So you've been making yourself sick?'

'Yes.' The tears were now rolling down his cheeks. 'But I'm always hungry. My job is quite physical. I'm always famished so I eat decent meals. And then I go and make myself sick; get rid of all the food.'

'You're making yourself ill.'

'I know.'

'When's the race?'

'At the Festival?'

'Yes.'

'Three months.'

'If you go on at this rate you won't be fit to race anyway.'

188

'I'm not getting any younger. There won't be any more chances.'

I listened to him for a while. His dream had always been to be a jockey but God had not been kind to him in making him so tall. It's difficult for young jockeys to make the weight when they are close to six feet tall. He knew, as well as I did, that a man who is over six feet tall and in his 40s can only make a good riding weight by making himself seriously ill.

'You have to tell Petronella.'

'I can't.'

'She's worried sick about your health. You can't not tell her. I suspect she probably thinks you've got cancer and that you're going to die.'

Farley looked at me in disbelief.

'Honestly,' I said. 'That's what she probably thinks.'

'Will you tell her?'

And so I called Petronella back into the consulting room and I told her that her husband had bulimia; that he was deliberately making himself sick so that he vomited up the food he'd eaten and didn't put on weight.

'Is this for that bloody race?' she asked me. 'That one they offered you at Cheltenham?'

He nodded. 'And there was talk of a ride at Aintree. In the Grand National.'

'You wouldn't have the strength to ride a horse round Aintree,' she told him. 'I've seen you struggle to get up the stairs.'

'Your heartbeat is irregular,' I told him. 'You really are making yourself ill. I very much doubt if the course doctors would let you ride. They'll see the same signs I've seen.'

Farley looked at me.

'How can you do this to yourself?' demanded Petronella. 'And to me? You're my whole life. If you kill yourself you'll leave a young, grieving widow. All over a bloody horse race.' The words came tumbling out, driven more by passion than anything else. And all the time Farley wept.

'It's what I always wanted to do,' he said at last. 'It was my dream.'

'I know it was,' said Petronella. She too was now crying. 'You're a great jockey. I know you are. I've seen you ride often enough. But you can't make the weight without making yourself ill. You're too tall, Farley. Lots of men would give their eye teeth to be six foot tall.'

'None of them jockeys,' said Farley, wryly.

I didn't expect that we would be able to persuade Farley to stop making himself vomit there and then. With commendable honesty he refused to give his word that he would stop. I offered to make him an appointment with a special clinic where he could see an expert. But he said he wouldn't go. He said he was too ashamed of what he was doing; too embarrassed to talk to a stranger about it.

So I told them both to come and see me together, twice a week. And twice a week I weighed him and checked his heart and looked at his hands and his teeth and his skin.

And I talked to a race course doctor I knew who told me that bulimia was a common problem among jockeys and that they were good at spotting it and that if a jockey was ill they would never let him climb aboard half a ton of thoroughbred horse and race over fences and hedges sometimes too high to see over.

When I told Farley what I knew, I also told him that I hadn't told the doctor the name of my patient. 'They don't know who you are. But race course doctors won't let you race in your condition.'

And slowly Farley came to terms with the fact that he could have a good life without risking his health trying to recapture something that had once seemed possible. He could still ride at Point to Point race meetings without making himself painfully thin. He had a wife who loved him dearly, a good home and a decent job.

One day the pair of them came in and Farley told me that he hadn't made himself sick for a month. He said he felt much better and that he had accepted that he was now never going to be a top jockey. He said that knowing that it was just his height that had thwarted his ambitions made it easier to accept.

'I'm a good jockey,' he said with quiet confidence. 'I could have been a winner.' And then, for the first time in weeks, he smiled and did a passable imitation of Marlon Brando. 'I could have been a contender,' he said, quoting Brando from the film *On the Waterfront*.

Petronella, smiling with him, put her arm around her husband and it was her turn to cry. 'I know you could,' she said softly. 'But if it's any consolation you won my heart long ago.'

'You're the one I always wanted to win,' said Farley.

I left them alone for a minute or two while I popped out to fetch a fresh box of paper tissues. I always keep a box of tissues on my desk but sometimes one box isn't enough.

Damnit, I needed a tissue myself.

Just to blow my nose you understand.

Tranny by Gaslight

I saw Donyard Hill most days when he cycled along the lane past Bilbury Grange.

He was usually headed to Peter Marshall's shop, to buy a pint of milk and a loaf of bread, though sometimes he cycled down into Combe Martin to treat himself and his wife to two pieces of cod and two bags of chips. He used to wrap the cod and the chips in an old coat to keep them warm before stuffing them into his saddlebag.

At the time, the chip shop in Combe Martin still wrapped the fish and chips in pieces of greaseproof paper which were then folded inside pages from old newspapers. To be honest, I don't think chips are really chips unless they are wrapped in old newspaper. To me they taste much better with a little newsprint wrapped round them than they do when sold in any of the alternative wrappers.

Moreover, I have always found that newspapers make fascinating reading when they are used as chip wrappers. Most chip shops used tabloid newspapers for the wrapping (the pages of a broadsheet were generally considered far too large) and many is the nugget of odd 'hey, listen to this' items of news I have found and enjoyed while eating my chips.

There's absolutely no entertainment value in plain, white wrapping paper or one of those hideous, plastic trays that are now considered acceptable by the health and safety gestapo.

Donyard is one of those people who were born well-equipped with silver spoons. He had one in his mouth and one in each of his little fists.

He seemed destined for greatness but, somehow, he never quite fulfilled the expectations of either parents or schoolteachers. He went to one of the top public schools and followed that with three years at Cambridge University where he read Politics, Philosophy and Economics.

'My tutors thought I'd have a career in politics but it never happened,' he told me with a shrug. 'I was the head boy at school so

I was doomed. Someone once told me that the majority of head boys and girls either end up as estate agents or in prison.'

Instead of a high-flying career in politics, Donyard decided to become a racing driver. That didn't turn out too well. His father wouldn't give him the money he needed to buy a good car and he never quite had the talent to obtain the sponsorship he needed. For a year or two, he worked as a press officer for one of the smaller racing teams. And then, when the team for which he was working went bust, he got a job as a car salesman. Customers liked the fact that he could talk about racing drivers he had met and circuits he had visited.

That career didn't last too long. Donyard was arrested for speeding and careless driving and lost his licence. The job went too. And so did his girlfriend he had met when he'd been a racing driver.

He told me all this one lunchtime in the Duck and Puddle, where he became a regular when he and his new wife, a lovely lady called Cynthia-Anne, moved into Bilbury and rented a small cottage just two hundred yards or so from the pub.

Donyard had managed to get himself appointed Club Secretary at the Kentisbury Golf Club. Cynthia-Anne, a gracile mignon, was at least one, and possibly two, generations younger than Donyard but they seemed very happy together. They had been married for a couple of years and had met at a Rock Music Festival on the Isle of Wight. They had a baby called Herman and a daft Dalmatian dog called Spot. Their tiny cottage had running water but no other utilities. In lieu of electricity, they had lamps and a cooker which all were fed with fuel from a liquefied gas cylinder. Their cottage was heated by a log burning stove which also provided them with hot water.

'Donyard's on the phone,' said Frank Parsons, landlord at the Duck and Puddle. 'He appears to have been arrested.'

It was early evening and Thumper Robinson, Patchy Fogg and I were having a pre-prandial libation while we discussed plans for the Bilbury Bonfire Night Party.

We take Bonfire Night very seriously in Bilbury. Mind you, we take most opportunities for celebration quite seriously. We celebrate the rise and fall of Guy Fawkes with a huge bonfire, as many fireworks as we can afford and a huge barbecue. It is never allowed to rain on bonfire night and if it does then we ignore the damp and carry on regardless.

I'm in charge of the bonfire since I have a well-earned reputation of being able to light a fire, and keep it burning, even if it is pouring with rain. One of my most magnificent bonfires was lit in a snowstorm. The fire burned steadily for several hours and I watched it from the comfort of my armchair in Bilbury Grange, popping out only occasionally to throw another pile of prunings onto the blaze. Patsy told her father about that bonfire and he told his wife and she told just about everyone else. My reputation as a maker of bonfires was sealed by that conflagration.

Startled, we all looked across at Frank.

'Arrested?' I said. 'What on earth for?'

Donyard was a breezy and colourful character but he wasn't the sort of fellow likely to get drunk, start a fight or steal sweets from F.W.Woolworth's emporium.

'He didn't say,' said Frank. He seemed slightly uncomfortable. 'I didn't like to ask him.' He muttered something about it not being the sort of thing you asked a fellow.

It seemed to me unlikely that Donyard would have telephoned just to let us know that he had been arrested. He obviously needed help of some sort. I jumped up, walked across to where Frank was standing and took the telephone from him.

'What's happened?' I asked.

'I've been arrested,' said Donyard. It didn't really sound like him. But it definitely was him. He sounded extremely nervous and frightened.

'What for?' I asked, cutting right to the chase, as I believe they say when making cowboy movies.

'Well, I wasn't actually doing anything,' said Donyard.

'They must have arrested you for something,' I said.

'It wasn't so much what I was doing,' he said, 'as what I'm wearing.'

'Why? What are you wearing?'

There was a long pause. I could hear someone in the background shouting to Donyard, telling him to hurry up and finish his call.

'A pink and lilac floral frock with a matching pink cardigan,' he said. 'Pink shoes and a little pink hat with two small feathers in it.'

'Pretty well covered the pink angle, then?'

'Pretty much.'

'And they've locked you up?'

'I was looking at the blouses in Marks and Spencer. A woman saw me and guessed I was a bloke dressed up. She went outside, found a copper and complained.'

'You weren't doing anything odd? Dancing around and singing something merry from Porgy and Bess for example?'

'No, no, not at all,' said Donyard, who was sounding a little more confident by the second. 'I was just there, looking at the blouses. You don't seem too shocked.'

'Why should I be shocked?'

'The woman who complained was shocked. The policeman who arrested me was shocked. Incidentally, the ironic thing is that the woman who complained about me was wearing jeans, Doc Martin boots and a plaid, woollen lumberjack shirt in orange and brown. If we'd swapped clothes no one would have said anything.'

'Tight-laced idiots the lot of them,' I said.

'Can I crave a boon?' said Donyard.

'Am I close if I guess you need bailing out?'

I wasn't in the slightest bit surprised to hear that there was another cross-dresser living in Bilbury. There are far more men who dress in feminine clothing than is generally realised. (Women can, and do, dress in male clothing without anyone noticing or thinking it in the slightest bit strange.) I had already met a villager called Montgomery Hall who liked to dress in the sort of clothing more commonly associated with women. He fell off his exercise bicycle and I helped his wife undress him, and clean the nail varnish off his nails before he went to hospital.

Since around one in ten men cross-dress from time to time, some wearing only feminine underwear and others dressing completely in feminine clothing, there were always bound to be numerous other cross-dressers or transvestites in the village.

I remember Montgomery Hall telling me that he had started by just wearing silky, feminine panties. 'I had no intention of ever wearing a bra,' he said. 'I just thought the panties felt better, more comfortable than itchy boxer shorts. But then, after a few months, I started to wear stockings and then I did add a bra and a slip and then, because I was a bachelor at the time, I started wearing a nightie. I had no intention of wearing a dress. After a while, I wouldn't go out of the house unless I was wearing a bra underneath my shirt, I felt half-dressed without one. And then I bought a skirt and a blouse in a charity shop and before I knew, I wondered where I could find a wig and some shoes that would fit.'

Another cross-dresser I spoke to said that he wore feminine clothing in the same way, and for the same reason, that Winston Churchill liked laying bricks. Churchill didn't want to be a bricklayer. He was just escaping from the stresses of his everyday life by being something else. Many transvestites feel like this and find that when wearing something flimsy and feminine they can allow themselves to be caring, emotional and gentle in a way that men aren't usually supposed to be. (I discovered from Donyard, by the way, that 'cisvestism' is the habit of dressing only in the clothes of one's own sex.)

'I'm afraid so,' said Donyard. 'Cynthia-Anne is at home looking after Herman but I couldn't ring her because we don't have a phone at the cottage. We've been waiting six months for British Telecom to install one.'

'Do you want me to tell her where you are?'

'Would you mind?'

'Of course not. Does she…er…know?'

'Know that I dress in women's clothing?'

'Yes.'

'Oh yes. She bought me the frock I'm wearing. It was a birthday present.'

'Good. That's good.' Suddenly, a thought occurred to me. 'What have you told the police?'

'I haven't told them anything.'

'You haven't made a statement?'

'No. I did mention that one day it will be just as reasonable for a man to walk round in a frock as it is for a woman to walk round in trousers.'

'What did the police say?'

'The snotty copper who arrested me said, 'Maybe, but this is the 1970s and it isn't legal now.'

'You didn't say anything else?'

'No. They haven't got round to asking me any questions yet. They just arrested me, giggled, and said a few rude things.'

'So they haven't charged you with anything?'

'No, not yet. I don't think they're quite sure what to charge me with. Do you know a good solicitor? '

'Don't tell them anything,' I told him. 'Just be indignant. We'll be with you shortly.'

'We?'

'Thumper and Patchy are here with me.'

'Of course,' said Donyard.

'And Donyard?'

'Yes?'

'A hat with two feathers in it?'

'It looks better than it sounds. Honest.'

'I hope so,' I told him. 'We'll be there shortly. Don't say anything and don't sign anything until we get there.'

I put down the telephone and turned to Thumper and Patchy. Thumper was finishing his pint of Old Restoration.

'Am I right in thinking that we are going somewhere?' said Patchy.

'We are,' I said. 'We're riding to the rescue of Donyard.' I explained why he had been arrested. Neither Thumper nor Patchy seemed shocked or even particularly surprised.

'Can't come with you, I'm afraid,' said Frank. 'Gilly is in Exeter. There's a meeting of the Licensed Victuallers' Association and it's her turn to go.'

'You stay here and hold the fort,' I told him. 'We will need refreshments when we return.'

Cynthia-Anne did not seem particularly surprised when we called in and explained what had happened to her husband. She was, however, clearly upset to hear that Donyard had been arrested. I'd have been worried if she hadn't been.

'He's been cross dressing for years,' she told us. 'But today was his first venture out in a dress. I did ask him not to go. Barnstaple doesn't look like a very broad-minded town to me.'

'Parts of it clearly aren't,' I told her.

'Will they send him to prison?' she asked, with tears in her eyes.

'Good heavens, no!' I replied. It seemed extremely unlikely.

'But it'll be in the local paper,' said Cynthia-Anne. 'And he'll lose his job. I can't see the committee at the Kentisbury Golf Club keeping him on as the Club Secretary, can you?'

'They probably wouldn't be over the moon about having a secretary in a pink hat with two feathers,' I agreed. 'But there may be a way out. Does Donyard have other feminine items in his wardrobe?'

'Oh yes,' replied Cynthia-Anne. 'He's got more feminine clothes than male clothes. When he's Donyard he only has a sports jacket and a couple of pairs of corduroy trousers. But when he's Molly he has a dozen dresses and skirts to choose from.'

'Molly?' said Patchy, puzzled. 'Who's Molly? Where did Molly come in?'

'Molly is what I call Donyard when he's dressed in feminine clothes,' explained Cynthia-Anne. She looked at us. 'Well, I can hardly call him Donyard when he's wearing a twin set and pearls can I?'

'No, I suppose not,' I agreed. 'But why Molly?'

'I don't have the foggiest idea why. I asked him and he doesn't know either. He's never known a Molly. I always thought it a rather pretty name.'

'And he has a twin set and pearls?'

'Oh yes. He looks lovely in it. It's a heather mixture in a tweedy sort of material. We found it in a charity shop in South Molton.'

And this a man whom no one could possibly describe as a pantywaist!

'Could you pop upstairs and collect some of Donyard's clothes?' I asked her. 'We'll need everything you can find. Including bras and stockings.'

Cynthia-Anne looked at me, puzzled.

'There's one way out of this,' I told her. 'If we turn up at the police station dressed as women and tell the police that we were all going to a fancy dress party they'll either have to arrest us all or let Donyard go.'

'You'd do that for him?' said Cynthia-Anne.

'We're going to do what?' demanded Thumper and Patchy simultaneously, as they realised what I'd just said.

'We just put on some of Donyard's gear and drive into Barnstaple and go to the police station,' I said. 'How hard is that? Not a lot to do for a chum, is it?'

Thumper and Patchy looked at each other.

'Actually, it's quite a lot,' said Thumper.

'Quite a lot,' agreed Patchy with a resigned sort of sigh.

'Fetch the clothes,' I told Cynthia-Anne. 'The quicker we get to Barnstaple, the quicker we get Donyard home.'

Cynthia-Anne disappeared up the stairs.

'I'm not wearing pink or anything too revealing,' called Thumper after her.

Two minutes later Cynthia-Anne was back downstairs with an armful of clothes and suitable underwear. By the time she returned, the three of us had stripped off down to our underpants. The Dalmation, clearly confused, had retreated and disappeared into the kitchen.

'I can't believe you're doing this for Donyard,' said Cynthia-Anne, laying the clothes out across the back of the sofa and two armchairs.

'Nor can I,' said Thumper.

'Oh, I like that one!' said Patchy, picking up a knee length frock in a darkish sky blue. He held the frock up against himself. 'Do you think it's my colour? I hope it will fit. You don't have anything in a powder blue, do you?'

Cynthia-Anne said she was sorry but that was the only blue frock that Donyard had in his wardrobe.

Fifteen minutes later, we were all dressed. Cynthia-Anne had showed us how to fasten stockings to our suspender belts, had fastened our bras for us and had provided rolled up socks and stockings to fill up our empty bra cups. Doing all this by gaslight was trickier than I would have imagined.

'Do you mean women have to go through all this every time they get dressed?' said Thumper, looking behind him to check that the seams on his stockings were straight.

'Do I look big enough?' demanded Patchy, adding another pair of socks to his bra. 'I don't want to go into town looking flat chested.'

'We'd better have some make-up on,' I told Cynthia-Anne. 'Give us some lipstick and a bit of stuff on our eyes.'

'Oh, come on!' said Thumper. 'Do we have to?'

'No point in spoiling the ship for a halfpenny's worth of tar,' said Patchy.

Cynthia-Anne made us up speedily. When she'd finished, I hardly recognised the other two.

'Lilac suits you,' I said to Thumper.

'Blue really is my colour,' said Patchy.

'Hair!' said Cynthia-Anne suddenly. 'You all need wigs.'

'Has Donyard got three spare wigs?' I asked her.

'No,' said Cynthia-Anne. 'He's only got one other wig. But I've got two party wigs. One in green and the other one in bright red.'

'I can't wear a green wig,' said Patchy instantly. 'Not with a blue dress.'

We squeezed our feet into three pairs of Donyard's shoes and eventually, gowned, made-up and wigged, we were ready to leave.

The three of us climbed into the Rolls-Royce and headed off for Barnstaple. 'The game's afoot!' cried Patchy, who seemed surprisingly confident considering our state of dress.

When we got to our destination, I parked the car next to a large No Unauthorised Parking sign in the police station car park and the three of us trooped into the reception area. I have always found that you can park an elderly Rolls-Royce almost anywhere you like without getting into much trouble.

The sergeant on the desk stared at us as if three Martians had landed and walked in.

'Good evening, sergeant,' I said politely. I made no effort to speak in a feminine voice. I'd tried doing that in the car as we drove to Barnstaple and I'd found that it was quite impossible.

'Evening, Madam,' said the sergeant. He swallowed and corrected myself. 'Er, Sir. Er, Sirs.'

I introduced myself and then introduced Thumper and Patchy. 'Four of us were on our way to a fancy dress party and I understand there's been some sort of silly mistake and you've accidentally arrested one of our number – Mr Donyard Hill.'

'A fancy dress party, doctor?'

'That's right. Haven't you heard about it? I think your Chief Constable is going to be there. I heard he was going as one of King Henry VIII's wives. Can't remember which one, though. Our wives have all gone ahead in another car. They're all dressed as vicars. Our friend is called Donyard Hill. He telephoned a little while ago to say that you'd arrested him for looking at blouses in Marks and Spencer's store.'

'Arrested him for looking at blouses?'

'I believe so,' I said. 'It seems a trifle heavy handed but maybe there's a new law come in about blouse browsing.'

A drunk who had been sitting on a chair in the reception area stood up, unsteadily, and came over to us. He tried to put his arm round Thumper.

'You're a pretty girl,' he said. 'Give us a kiss.'

Thumper glared at him. Patchy, guessing what was in Thumper's mind and thinking that it might not be a good idea to floor a stranger in a police station, held onto his arm.

'Sit down, sunbeam!' hissed Thumper. 'Or you'll be digesting your teeth.'

The drunk quickly edged away and sat down on the floor. He then crawled back to the chair on which he had been sitting and tried to look as small and as insignificant as possible.

'This is a shocking thing,' said Patchy. 'Mr Hill is a very eminent member of the community. A very distinguished man, you know.'

'He didn't say anything about a party, sir,' said the police sergeant, defensively.

'Probably thought it wasn't any of your business,' said Patchy.

'I expect he just wanted to see how far you'd go with this,' I said. 'He's probably planning to make a formal complaint about how the police in Barnstaple harass ordinary members of the public.' I paused. 'Can I have your name, sergeant?'

'Evans, doctor,' said the sergeant. 'Sergeant Evans, sir. I think there's probably just been a bit of a mistake, sir. Just give me a minute, please, doctor.'

He hurried off. I noticed him talking to a young police constable who was trying to grow a moustache. It looked as if it was hard going.

A minute or so later, he returned with Donyard following him.

'Ah there you are,' I cried. 'We lost you in town. But we're still not too late for the party.'

'Thank heavens for that,' said Donyard, catching on fast. 'I'd have hated to miss the party.'

'The chief constable said he'd reserved the first dance with you,' said Thumper to Donyard. 'Your left boob has slipped. They haven't been molesting you, have they?'

Donyard looked down and adjusted the contents of his left bra cup.

I glowered at Thumper. 'Are there any charges, sergeant?' I asked the policeman. 'The three of us haven't been looking at blouses but

201

do you perhaps want to arrest the rest of us?' I have always found that it pays to be polite but firm when dealing with the constabulary. And a little arrogant sarcasm, delivered from a height, never seems to do much harm.

'No, no, there are no charges at all,' said the sergeant quickly. 'Apologies, sir, for the inconvenience and the misunderstanding.' He lifted the flap in the desk so that Donyard could leave.

'Saved by the three Paladins!' murmured Donyard.

We walked out of the police station, our heels click-clacking on the linoleum, and made our way to the car. I realised that my hands were shaking.

'Is this your car, sir?' asked a policeman who was standing next to it. It was the young policeman who was trying to grow a moustache. He looked about 15 and I realised I was getting old.

I said it was.

'I've just been looking after it for you, sir,' said the policeman. 'Some of our drivers are a bit careless when they're parking. The sergeant didn't want anyone denting your vehicle.'

We climbed in and settled ourselves. I managed to stop my hands shaking before I backed out of the car park. The 15-year-old policeman with the junior moustache held up the traffic so that we could leave the car park without having to wait for a break in the flow of cars, vans and lorries. I waved an imperious thank you. Thumper, who always likes to push things as close to the edge as he can, blew the policeman a kiss. Patchy said the policeman looked embarrassed and swore that he was blushing.

And then we drove home to Bilbury.

After telling Cynthia-Anne that we had rescued her husband, and that there were to be no charges, we retired to the Duck and Puddle where Donyard was in charge of buying drinks for the evening.

Frank said that he thought that blue really suited Patchy and that my green hair and off the shoulder red dress were really eye catching. When Frank didn't say anything about him, Thumper got quite upset. Frank then told Thumper that he had the most impressive bosom but that if he had to make a criticism he would say that the whole construction did look to be rather on the lumpy side. Thumper said that this might be because in order to obtain the best possible effect, he had stuffed each bra cup with three pairs of rolled up socks and a woollen glove.

'Why are you wearing eye make-up?' asked Patsy when I got home later that evening.

'It's another long story…'

'I would imagine it is!'

'You're not going to believe it…'

Patsy smiled and looked at me. 'Most people probably wouldn't. But I know I will because more odd things happen to you than anyone else I know.'

'Well,' I began, 'Thumper, Patchy and I were sitting quietly in the snug at the Duck and Puddle…'

'That's how most of your bizarre stories start.'

'Be quiet and listen…'

'OK. Sorry.'

'Thumper, Patchy and I were sitting quietly in the snug at the Duck and Puddle…'

Appendix 1:

More Obscure Medical Words

In my book 'The Young Country Doctor Book 8: Bilbury Tonic' I included a list of obscure medical words which my GP friend William and I had compiled.

William and I have always been fascinated by words – especially medical words and quasi medical words – and when we were students together we would waste rare evenings in the local pub looking up and memorising examples of obscure medical terminology.

As far as we were concerned, the more obscure the word the more we liked it. William had a Victorian dictionary which we scoured for new examples. And since I am a bibliotaph and suffer from chronic bibliolatry I have, over the years, acquired an embarrassingly large collection of dictionaries, books of quotations and thesauruses.

The first rule was that although the words which we selected had to be heard or read only rarely, they had to be quite real – proper words rather than made-up words.

The second rule was that a word would not count unless the person offering it could both spell it and pronounce it.

Here is another list of obscure (mostly) medical words which William and I compiled together during one of his regular and welcome visits to Bilbury:

Adscititious – supplementary, additional
Agerasia – youthful appearance in old person
Ataraxia – serene calmness
Bezzle – (traditional) to drink and to behave sottishly
Bifarious – facing both ways, someone who will support anything
Braxy – meat taken from a sheep that has fallen dead or had an accident
Bustluscious – having shapely breasts

Callipygian – having shapely buttocks
Cisvestism – habit of dressing only in the clothes of one's own sex
Cockalorum – little man with a high opinion of himself
Coryza – runny nose, common cold
Cotquean – a man doing a woman's work
Crapulous – hangover
Crinkum-crankum – fussy, over decorated things
Curmudgeon – bad tempered or surly person
Daphlean – shy and beautiful
Dander – a show of temper
Dandiprat – anything small
Demergature – death by drowning
Demi-lass – a polite word for a trollop, slut or slag
Demirep – someone with no reputation at all
Doliochocnemic – having long legs
Doliochoproscopic – having a long and narrow face
Ecdysiast –a snake sloughing its skin but also a strip tease practitioner
Eesome – pleasing to the eye
Exoptable – very desirable
Fettle – to mend, repair
Frample – peevish or sour
Franion – licentious person,
Fushionless – insipid, feeble
Gallimaufry – a jumble or medley of things
Galliard – man of fashion
Gangrel – loafing lout
Gracile – slender and graceful
Gripple – mean or stingy
Gruntle – continuous lamentation
Hirple – to limp, slow and painful motion
Hornswoggle – to cheat
Horbgorble – to putter about in an ineffective way
Imposthume – a boil
Kittle – to tickle
Leesome – lovable
Leptosome – having a pleasingly slender body
Lungis – a tall and clumsy man
Lusk – sloth

Lubricious – slippery or intended to arouse sexual desire
Macromastia – very large breasts
Maltworm – a drinker
Megrim – headache, migraine
Miffy – a fit of peevish ill humour
Mignon - dainty
Moonling – a dreamy fool
Muckender –handkerchief
Muffish – soft and effeminate
Mugwump – someone who backs down, withdraws
Mulligrub – a depression
Mumchance – silent or tongue tied
Myrmidon – unscrupulous follower
Oddling – the lonely, strange
Oleaginous – oily
Pantywaist – effeminate or feeble
Poculation – drinking alcohol
Poltroon – a coward
Pulchritudinous – comely
Scobberlotcher – an idler
Scurryfunge – an old-fashioned toothbrush, stiff hooked article
Slaister – to slap on make-up in a wanton sort of way
Slammerkin – slattern, and the loose covering she may wear
Sloomy – spiritless and dull
Spawling – a noisy clearing of the throat
Tiddle – to fidget
Tittup – someone with a mincing, prancing gait
Titivil – a knave or a trivial piece of gossip
Toralium – eiderdown
Toilet – was originally the cloth used for wrapping clothes, or a towel placed around the shoulders by a barber, then it became the linen covering of a dressing table, then the word was used to denote the dressing table and all the stuff on it and, finally, it became an alternative to 'lavatory'
Toothsome –voluptuous and alluring
Tretis – well-proportioned and graceful
Trollop – sluttish woman
Trollope – loose garment, a carelessly worn wrapper

Uncumber – disencumber (St Uncumber – was a bearded woman and benefactress of wives, according to Sir Thomas More – for a peck of oats she would provide a horse upon which an evil husband could ride to the devil)

Usky, usquebaugh – whisky

Vapours – supposed to be exhalations from the organs rising to affect the brain and agitating the nervous system (in Victorian times individuals, usually female, who were upset, faint or nervous were said to be suffering from an attack of the vapours)

Venust – beautiful and elegant

Venecund – shy and bashful

Vilipend – to hold cheap or think poorly of someone

Viritoot – a spree or jaunt

Wanhope – despair

Wanton – ungoverned, rebellious

Zenonian – obstinate

Zest – eagerness

If the organisers of the Olympics are looking for a new and slightly more intellectual attraction than weight lifting or pole vaulting, maybe they could introduce an event requiring competitors to squeeze a selection of the words above into a single sentence. The gold medal would go to the individual who managed to get the most words between an initial capital and a final full stop. But the sentence would, of course, have to be grammatically acceptable and to make (some sort of) sense.

Appendix 2

Are You A NOD Or A BOAJ?

Doctors often use a private code when writing medical notes about patients.

They do it partly to save time and partly so that patients won't know what they have written.

Just in case you get a chance to look at your medical records here are some of the abbreviations which are most commonly used these days.

(Though do remember that not all these abbreviations are used by all doctors or in all hospitals).

NOD – Nice old duck

ACD – A complete dickhead

FAS – Fat and silly

NQOC – Not quite our class

RATTPO – Reassured and told to piss off

SITH – Soft in the head

BOAJ – Bit of a jerk

KSI – Knows someone important

PITB – Pain in the bum

SAD – Smelly and demented

GOK – God only knows

If you find these abbreviations as offensive as I do why not fight back.

Here are two sets of abbreviations that you could try scribbling against your doctor's name in retaliation:

JUSLTIAWC – Jumped up spotty little twerp in a white coat

POFIAS – Pompous old fart in a suit

I'm sure you'll be able to think of more...

Appendix 3

A Hamper of Assistants

In the piece in this book entitled *Charcoal and Geese*, I explained that a flock of geese on land is known as a gaggle but that the geese mysteriously become a wedge or a skein when they start to fly. Everyone knows that a collection of fish is a shoal and that a group of birds a flock. Most people know that groups of dogs, horses and cattle are collectively known as a pack, a string and a herd. It's quite well known that a group of spiders are known as a smother. Collective nouns for goldfish, ravens and doves are a trembling, an unkindness and a pitying.

But, over 30 years ago, it occurred to me that no one had previously created collective nouns for specific, groups of people.

And so I constructed an original list of collective nouns for a book I wrote under the pen name of Edward Vernon.

I have been constantly adding to my list.

A few years ago, I included a list in one of my published diaries. But the list is forever growing.

So, here is my new, improved and expanded list of collective nouns for humans:

A hamper of assistants
A congregation of clergymen
A galaxy of actresses
A pride of expectant fathers
A knot of scouts
A shower of weather forecasters
A swarm of heating engineers
A congestion of children
A clump of labourers
A drove of chauffeurs
A clutch of car mechanics

A collection of philatelists
A ring of proctologists
A batch of cooks
A press of laundrymen
A girdle of corsetieres
A quantity of surveyors
A parcel of postmen
A cast of sculptors
A band of rubber workers
A tuft of trichologists
A wealth of publishers
A stream of urologists
An embarrassment of parents
A flourish of magicians
A cluster of diamond cutters
A ring of jewellers
A posse of vets
A flounce of divas
A bunch of florists
A nest of mothers
A stack of booksellers/librarians
A corps of pathologists
A cup of bra makers
A congress of prostitutes
A concentration of students
A body of undertakers
A chest of transvestites
A company of representatives
A set of osteopaths
A dossier of policemen
A sheaf of administrators
A pile of gastroenterologists
An aggregation of biochemists
An association of psychologists
A drift of skiers
A clutch of physiotherapists
A school of nurses
A meeting of social workers
A herd of audiologists

A convergence of opticians
An issue of journalists
A brood of midwives
A community of public health officials
A cell of cytologists
A branch of foresters
A line of geneticists
A chain of chemists
A growth of endocrinologists
A cloud of spiritualists
A catch of obstetricians
A smear of laboratory technicians
A promenade of chiropodists
A gathering of dress makers
A camaraderie of photographers
A host of bacteriologists
An order of waiters
A pyramid of archeologists
A giggle of teenage girls
A gawp of teenage boys
A hold of sailors
A grip of luggage handlers
A slump of economists
A grievance of defendants
A whinge of consumers
A bore of mining engineers
A pot of painters
A nerd of IT workers
A bosom of strippers
A blush of nudists
A strut of models
A welcome of receptionists
An embarrassment of drunks

Appendix 4

Medical Abbreviations: how to read your prescription (and your medical notes)

Doctors like to use a good many Latin abbreviations when writing prescriptions or medical notes. The truth (speak it softly) is that most don't know much Latin and probably don't understand the real meaning of the abbreviations they use with such brio.

But here are the commonest dog Latin medical abbreviations and their meanings. Refer to this list if you need to translate your medical notes or the break the code doctors use when writing prescriptions.

Ac – before meals
Ad lib – freely
Alt die – alternate days
Bd – twice daily
C – with
Cap – capsule
c/o – complains of
dc – discontinue
ddx – differential diagnosis
dnr – do not resuscitate
dol urg – when the pain is severe
-ectomy – any word ending in ectomy suggests a removal operation
(such as appendicetomy or tonsillectomy)
fx – fracture
gutt – drops
hs – bedtime
im – intramuscularly
in vitro – in the lab
in vivo – in the patient
iv - intravenously

jt – joint
lbp –low back pain
llq – left lower quadrant of the abdomen
luq – left upper quadrant of the abdomen
m – mix
n/v – nausea and or vomiting
npo – nothing by mouth
od – right eye
om – every morning
on – evening evening
os – left eye
- oscopy – a word ending in oscopy suggests having a looking at
something inside the body (as in bronchoscopy, which means having
a look inside the lungs or laparoscopy which means taking a look
inside the abdomen)
- ostomy – a word ending in ostomy suggests that an artificial hole
has been made (as a colostomy, in which a hole is made in the colon)
-otomy – a word ending in otomy suggests that an incision will be
made (as in laparotomy, which means an incision in the abdomen)
ou – both eyes
p – pulse
-plasty – a word ending in plasty suggests a plastic surgeon
operation (such as mammoplasty, which means a redesign of breast
shape or size)
po – orally
prn - as required
qd – four times daily
qid – four times daily
qam – mornings
qhs – bedtime
r – prescribe
rlq – right lower quadrant of abdomen
ruq – right upper quadrant of abdomen
sob – shortness of breath
sos – if necessary
sq – subcutaneous
stat – immediately
t – temperature
t&a – tonsillectomy and adenoidectomy

tab – tablet
td – three times a day
tds – three times a day
tid – three times a day
thr –total hip replacement
tkr –total knee replacement
ua – urine analysis
ung – ointment
uri – upper respiratory tract infection
uti –urinary tract infection
vss – vital signs stable (pulse, temperature, blood pressure are stable)
wt – weight

And finally (once again)…

I hope you have enjoyed this book about Bilbury and the people who live in and visit the village. If you did so then I would be very grateful if you would spare a moment to write a short review. This is the 12th book in the series entitled 'The Young Country Doctor'.
Thank you
Vernon Coleman

Made in the USA
Middletown, DE
20 May 2021